Praise for *Think Like Zuck*

"Ekaterina writes about innovation not only from the heart but also with the wisdom that comes from having led Intel through a social media transformation. Read this book—and buy it for the budding innovators in your company to inspire their passion and purpose."

—**Charlene Li**, author of bestsellers *Open Leadership* and *Groundswell* and founder of Altimeter Group

"*Think Like Zuck* provides a fresh perspective on entrepreneurship, drawing inspiration from some of the most innovative companies of our time."

—**Clara Shih**, author of *The Facebook Era: Tapping Online Social Networks to Market, Sell, and Innovate*

"*Think Like Zuck* is a fascinating look at how entrepreneurial vision drives success. If you want more out of work than just a job, if you have the burning desire to build something of lasting value, then this is your guide. It's for harnessing an entrepreneurial spirit no matter where you are—on your own, inside a big company, or as part of a nonprofit, church, or any other organization."

—**David Meerman Scott**, bestselling author of *The New Rules of Marketing and PR*

"Ekaterina Walter does far more than reveal the story of Facebook and its founder, Mark Zuckerberg. She reveals the emotional, intellectual, and proactive blueprint that determines which entrepreneurs fail, which succeed, and the few that do so spectacularly. *Think Like Zuck* is a must read for any innovator, social entrepreneur, or business owner looking to capitalize on the success of Facebook to propel and realize their own vision."

—**Simon Mainwaring**, *New York Times* bestselling author of *We First: How Brands and Consumers Use Social Media to Build a Better World*

"*Think Like Zuck*'s thoughtful rendering of the Facebook phenomenon provides keen insight into the one thing that the most successful companies on the web share: an ability to create instant and vital connections among individuals around the world. In its rapid spread to give us all both a global soapbox *and* a virtual fence to chat and share pictures over, Facebook represents a fundamental shift in the way we live: the Internet is now the primary touch point for the relationships people form. Businesses with an eye on profit must read this book and come to terms with the undeniable reality of Mark Zuckerberg's vision."

—**Keith Ferrazzi**, founder and chairman of Ferrazzi Greenlight
and *New York Times* bestselling author of
Who's Got Your Back and *Never Eat Alone*

Think Like
Zuck

Think Like Zuck

The Five Business Secrets of

Facebook's Improbably Brilliant CEO Mark Zuckerberg

Ekaterina Walter

NEW YORK   CHICAGO   SAN FRANCISCO
LISBON   LONDON   MADRID   MEXICO CITY   MILAN
NEW DELHI   SAN JUAN   SEOUL   SINGAPORE
SYDNEY   TORONTO

The *McGraw·Hill* Companies

1 2 3 4 5 6 7 8 9 10   DOC/DOC   1 8 7 6 5 4 3 2

ISBN 978-0-07-180949-8
MHID   0-07-180949-X

e-ISBN 978-0-07-180950-4
e-MHID   0-07-180950-3

McGraw-Hill books are available at special quantity discounts to use as premiums and sales promotions or for use in corporate training programs. To contact a representative, please e-mail us at bulksales@mcgraw-hill.com.

This book is printed on acid-free paper.

To all the dreamers: it is because you refuse to recognize the "impossible" that breathtaking innovation happens.

To my father, Oleg. Your self-sacrifice and guidance have helped shape my future.

CONTENTS

Acknowledgments

First and foremost, I would like to thank you, the reader, for picking up this book. I do hope you will find everything you are looking for inside. Your thoughts are welcome at www.ekaterinawalter.com.

My deepest gratitude to Dave Kerpen and Stephanie Frerich for propelling me to make my dream of writing a book a reality. I am blessed to call you both friends.

My appreciation to Facebook's founders and its leadership for building a company worth writing about.

Thanks to Ricky Van Veen, Jake Nickell, Aric Wood, David Armano, Scott Monty, Leslie Bradshaw, Jane Price, Nancy Bhagat, and Michelle Kaiser for your contributions to this project. It was a privilege to work with you. Special acknowledgments to Ellen McGirt and David Kirkpatrick for their wisdom and historic accounts of Facebook's growth. Big thanks to the XPLANE team for taking my scattered thoughts and putting them into appealing visuals. It has been a gratifying experience to work with the amazing team at McGraw-Hill: Stephanie Frerich, Pamela Peterson, Laura Yieh, and Mary Glenn.

I am thankful to all my friends who encouraged and supported me throughout the years and especially in the launch of this book. You are a gift!

Although my family is last in these acknowledgments, they come first in my life. My success and personal growth wouldn't be possible if not for their love and support. Eternal gratitude goes to: my husband, Brian, for being the best friend and partner anyone could wish for; my father, Oleg, for his courage, for showing me what's possible, and for being the sounding board for the ideas and concepts in this book; my mother, Valentina, for her complete and undying faith in me; my sister, Natalia, for always being there for me; my grandparents, Taya and Vladimir, for their wisdom and strength; my in-laws, Lauri and Ray, for accepting me and loving me like their own; and my aunt, Ludmila, for her unconditional love. And a big warm hug goes to my little daughter, Taya, who teaches me how to be a kid again every single day.

Think Like Zuck

INTRODUCTION

CONNECTING THE WORLD

This morning, there are more than one billion people using Facebook actively each month. If you're reading this: thank you for giving me and my little team the honor of serving you. Helping a billion people connect is amazing, humbling and by far the thing I am most proud of in my life. I am committed to working every day to make Facebook better for you, and hopefully together one day we will be able to connect the rest of the world too.

—Mark Zuckerberg in his Facebook status update

on October 4, 2012[1]

It was a priceless gift. A gift of life. And it wasn't Santa Claus who brought it right before Christmas 2010. It was Facebook.

Donette Warren was desperate. Her ten-year-old daughter, Vivica, badly needed a kidney transplant. She had been on dialysis for three years, 12 hours a night. It was very hard to watch and harder for the little girl's body to endure. Donette, a mother of five from Minnesota, took to Facebook to help spread the word and get her child badly needed help. She posted on Facebook again and again, pleading with her friends to share and repost on their walls. She was looking for a miracle.

And she got it. Cathy Olsen, a total stranger, saw the post on her friend's Facebook page. She had three kids of her own, and her heart went out to the little girl. That night, she showed the post to her family and told them she wanted to help. They approved. Cathy had never been through surgery, but she didn't hesitate. Since family members are not automatically considered matches, Cathy knew she would probably never be able to contribute a kidney to one of her own children. Cathy was tested and determined a match for Vivica. So she went ahead and gave up her kidney at the University of Minnesota on November 17. "I couldn't sit around and watch a girl die that I knew I was a match for," she said. "I hope she's having the best Christmas ever!"

Vivica is all smiles; she is practically pain-free. "Freedom," she says. "[Cathy] is my angel."

Her mom agrees: "How many people have one of those?"[2]

This is a true storybook holiday miracle. And it happened because of the connections that Facebook facilitates among people of different ages, genders, backgrounds, and locations.

There have been many touching stories like Vivica's ever since Facebook launched on February 4, 2004. There are also stories about triumphs of love, as in the case of Paul Eaton and Dawn Pitman. In their twenties, the couple enjoyed an 18-month romance before going their separate ways.

They continued to think about each other through the years until, 27 years later, Paul decided to join Facebook. Paul remembers: "I had only been on Facebook for a day. I just typed Dawn's name in and hoped for the best."

Dawn's niece, Rachel, had put up their holiday pictures on Facebook, which Dawn didn't approve of: "The irony was that I told her to take them off because I felt it was an invasion of privacy, and she said she would get around to it when she had time. That's when Paul got in touch."

The couple met up on New Year's Eve 2008, and they were quite pleased to discover they hadn't changed much. They both liked the same things, drove the same cars, and remembered each other fondly. The rekindled connection was quite instant. "I knew then he was the one for me," said Dawn.[3]

Then there's the story of the man and woman with the same name who got married after meeting through Facebook. A young man from Texas, Kelly Hildebrandt, and a young woman from Florida, also named Kelly Hildebrandt, thought it was kind of amusing that they had the same first and last names and started a casual conversation on the topic. Eight months later—thanks to "love at Facebook sight"—Kelly proposed to Kelly, and the rest is history.[4]

Then there are the stories of reunited families, such as Don Gibson finding his son after 21 years. Don was a U.S. airman when he met Chrissie in the United Kingdom. They married in 1989 and had a son, Craig. Don was forced to move back to the United States to continue his Air Force service. Chrissie stayed behind, as she had two other sons from her previous marriage. They tried to stay in touch, but after a while, they lost contact with each other. For years, father and son looked for one another until one day Don logged onto Facebook and found Craig's half-brother and, through him, Craig. The two reunited on Skype before Father's Day 2012. The romance between Don and Chrissie rekindled. "We can be a family again," said Don. "I thank my lucky stars for modern technology, because without that, we wouldn't be here."[5]

Family reunification pages started to appear on Facebook after natural disasters like earthquakes and tornados and other deadly events like shootings to help facilitate connections between survivors and provide support.

And then there are stories of saved businesses. These days, Bistro 17, a small French-themed restaurant on Hilton Head Island, South Carolina, is always buzzing with customers. Besides boasting mouthwatering Brie, the restaurant is dog-friendly, with dog bowls and treats on hand (and yes, they even have a puppy menu). But the place wasn't always brimming with excitement. At one point, Bistro 17 was on the brink of shutting down. Anna Buckingham, the owner, tends to make friends with her customers. A partnership with one regular patron—who ran a Hilton Head Island Facebook page with over 65,000 fans—saved the business. They teamed up and created a great list of promotional ideas to help spread the word about Bistro 17 and rally the community around worthwhile causes.[6]

There are also stories of:

- Ben Saylor, a 17-year-old boy who turned to the social networking site to organize a community effort to rebuild the Pioneer Playhouse, the oldest outdoor theater in Kentucky, after it was damaged in a flood.

- Danish Prime Minister Anders Fogh Rasmussen, who, during his time in office, went jogging with a hundred of his Facebook fans.

- Holly Rose, whose friend's Facebook status update urging women to check for breast cancer allowed Holly to be diagnosed in time to treat the disease.[7]

- Men and women around the world who have used Facebook to create powerful movements for causes such as freedom from oppression, freedom of speech, human rights, and animal rights.

Mark Zuckerberg, the founder and CEO of Facebook, says in one of his blog posts: "Our mission is to help make the world more open and connected. Stories like these are examples of that mission and are both humbling and inspiring."[8]

Indeed! Such stories reflect a fundamental societal shift in which technologies are empowering us (and in some instances even saving our lives). We live in the era of digital revolution. Everyone can now have a voice; an individual can now be an authority. And social networks have the ability to give us true power of identity, to make our voices stronger, and, most important, to provide a platform for our voices to be heard. And Facebook is the biggest platform of them all.

In eight years of existence, Facebook has fundamentally changed the way we interact online. It is the world's largest enabler of human communication. We cannot imagine our lives without Facebook—it created a sweet addiction of 24/7 connection and information flow that we apparently all craved. We check Facebook before we go to bed and first thing in the morning when we wake up. It allows us to show the world our own unique identities, our own brands. It allows us to tell our stories, stories that can be heard at scale. It allows us to build global communities and rally around causes we are passionate about, enabling energized citizens to turn themselves into activists. Our News Feeds have become our personalized digital newspapers. And instead of picking up a phone, we log into Facebook to see what our friends are up to, check out pictures they recently posted, look at product recommendations (or complaints) they shared, or see what music they are currently listening to.

Paul Adams, the global brand experience manager at Facebook, describes this seismic shift the best: "[The web is] moving away from being built around content and is being rebuilt around people."[9]

Facebook was founded by 19-year-old Mark Elliot Zuckerberg (or Zuck, as he is known to every one of his acquaintances) on February 4, 2004. At the time, Zuck was a student at Harvard University, majoring in computer science and sociology. He first started the network with the purpose of connecting Harvard students. When non-Harvard students expressed interest, he expanded Facebook to more schools and, later, to the rest of the world. When users showed enormous interest and the network started to grow, Zuck dropped out of college and moved to Palo Alto, California, to solely focus on the endeavor. Facebook's success made him a billionaire at 23.

Here is the company's history at a glance and some notable milestones:

- In 2004, Zuckerberg starts Facebook with the help of his friends Chris Hughes, Dustin Moskovitz, and Eduardo Saverin. After three weeks, the site had more than 6,000 users. After opening to other colleges, the site grows to 10,000 users in one month and to over 30,000 in two months. In September 2004, Zuckerberg names Sean Parker president of the company. By then they have over 200,000 users. Parker goes on to play a critical role in Facebook's expansion and acquiring financial backing.[10]

- The same year, Facebook receives its first-ever investment (besides some initial investment by cofounders): $500,000 from Peter Thiel, cofounder of PayPal and a private investor, and $40,000 from Reid Hoffman, the founder of LinkedIn and an angel investor.[11]

- In September 2004, Facebook introduces two of the most critical site improvements: "the Wall" and Groups. The Wall becomes an instant hit.

- By end of November 2004, the site hits one million users.[12]

- By October 2005, the site reaches five million users, with 65 percent returning daily and 90 percent returning at least one a week. Users view 230 million pages daily, and revenue from ads climbs to $1 million/month.[13]

- In 2005, the Accel Partners venture capital firm agrees to invest $12.7 million in the venture, a deal that values Facebook at about $98 million postinvestment. This type of evaluation is unheard of at the time; even Google's first large investment valued the company at less than $75 million.[14]

- The company officially becomes Facebook on September 20, 2005.

- In fall 2005, Facebook introduces one of its most successful and critical features—photos with tagging ability. By late 2010, Facebook will be hosting 40 billion photos, making it the largest photo-sharing site.[15]

- On September 5, 2006, News Feed launches. It is the most controversial and most critical product update in the history of Facebook.

- In September 2006, Facebook opens up to everyone. By the end of 2006, the company has 12 million active users.[16]

- On May 24, 2007, at the very first Facebook developer conference, f8, the company announces that it is officially a platform and demonstrates its first apps with a handful of partners. Six months later, 250,000 developers are registered operating 25,000 applications, and half of Facebook users have at least one application on their profile.[17]

- As of May 2007, Facebook reaches 24 million active users, with 150,000 joining every day.[18]

- In November 2007, Facebook announces Beacon, a new social advertising system. The product causes one of the worst controversies Facebook will ever face and is shut down in 2009.

- By mid-2008, Facebook has over 100 million active users.[19]

- In July 2008, Facebook Connect launches.

- In 2008, *Time* names Zuckerberg one of the world's most influential people.

- In 2009, *Fast Company* ranks Facebook number 15 in its annual list of the world's 50 most innovative companies.

- By September 2009, Facebook reaches 200 million users.[20]

- In January 2009, Facebook passes MySpace to become the top social network/blog site, a position it has held in the United States ever since.[21]

- Between 2005 and 2009, Facebook doubles its traffic each year in the United States, surpassing 10 million unique visitors for the first time in November 2006 (11.6 million).[22]

- In 2010, the Open Graph API launches.

- Facebook.com becomes the number-one ranked website in the United States in March 2010.[23]

- In April 2010, Facebook launches the Like button.[24]

- By July 2010, Facebook reaches 300 million users.[25]

- In 2010, Mark Zuckerberg is named *Time*'s "Person of the Year."

- By September 2011, Facebook reaches 800 million users.[26]

- In 2011, Facebook overtakes Orkut as the top social networking site in Brazil.[27]

- In the fall of 2011, Facebook introduces Timeline, a new format of the personal page that creates a catalog of your life's moments. It is one of the most major site redesigns since the introduction of News Feed. In early 2012, Facebook rolls out Timeline to all brand pages.

- By April 2012, Facebook reaches 900 million users.[28]

- On May 17, 2012, Facebook raises $16 billion in an initial public offering that values the company at $104 billion. It is the third-largest public offering in U.S. history, behind General Motors and Visa. At that evaluation, the company's market value is higher than all but a handful of American companies, such as McDonald's, Citigroup, Amazon.com, and Goldman Sachs. Going public makes Zuck the twenty-ninth richest person in the world (according to Bloomberg's Billionaires Index).

- In September 2012, Facebook reaches one billion users.

There are about seven billion people in the world, two billion of whom are on the Internet. And half of those Internet users are on Facebook, which represents one-seventh of the world population. According to socialbakers .com, a monitoring service that tracks Facebook statistics and user metrics, as of August 2012, Facebook's number of users on each continent and its population penetration stood at:[29]

- North America: 228 million (43 percent)

- Europe: 242 million (30 percent)

- Asia: 235 million (6 percent)

- South America: 130 million (33 percent)

- Africa: 44 million (5 percent)

- Australia and Oceania: 14 million (41 percent)

No social network has ever commanded a greater global share of Internet users, their attention, or their shared media. Facebook became the platform of choice for scrapbooking lovers, political candidates, major brands, and artists, all looking to engage with their friends, fans, and communities. This is a true platform for two-way dialogue instead of one-way broadcasting.

Facebook became an integral part of the web's DNA and now lords over the digital landscape with no pretenders in sight. With one billion users worldwide, it is the largest global social media site. To put this into perspective, consider that the largest international broadcast network, the BBC World Service, reaches 188 million people on a weekly basis.[30] This pales in comparison to the daily reach of Facebook. According to statistics issued by Facebook on March 2012, there are on average 526 million daily active users on the site.[31]

Facebook is a social network, a media channel, and an identity system. Our Facebook profile (which tells others what we care about and who we trust) is becoming the Internet equivalent of a passport, a way to verify our identity online. Websites invite us to log in using a Facebook ID, and it moves with us from website to website. According to Janrain, a provider of social login services, Facebook owns identity on the Internet. In its second quarter 2012 study, Janrain found that 48 percent of users prefer logging into third-party sites using Facebook, followed by Google (30 percent) and Twitter (9 percent).[32]

Facebook offers brands and advertisers a global platform to reach their current and potential customers, with the exception of China, where Facebook doesn't operate. Facebook is now the epicenter of marketers' digital campaigns, from display ads to brand pages. As a platform, Facebook created a whole new set of economic opportunities allowing third parties to build valuable extensions to the way individuals and businesses interact online.

Here are a few additional interesting data points that speak to Facebook's status as a powerhouse:

- If Facebook were a country, it would be the third largest in the world, behind only China and India. Facebook is available in more than 70 languages.[33] Internationally, Facebook.com ranks among the top two websites in every market except China.[34]

- Facebook accounts for one in every seven minutes spent online around the world and three in every four social networking minutes.[35]

- 543 million monthly active users use Facebook mobile products.[36]

- Almost one billion pieces of content are shared on Facebook daily from an Open Graph.[37]

- Facebook is a dominant photo player on an increasingly visual Internet, with more than 300 million photos uploaded to the site per day.[38]

- There are more than 42 million active brand and celebrity pages (with 10 or more likes).[39]

- 24.3 percent of the top 10,000 websites in the world have some form of official Facebook integration on their home pages. And if you include regular links to Facebook, the number soars to 49.3 percent.[40]

- In the United States, one in every five Internet page views occurs on Facebook.com.[41] "Facebook" is the most searched term, and Facebook-related terms account for 14 percent of the top search clicks.[42]

So how did the social networking site become what Zuckerberg himself describes as "the most powerful distribution mechanism that's been created in a generation"?[43] This book will explore the answers to that question. We will take a walk down history's lane to uncover the success secrets of Facebook's triumph. We will look at its leader, his vision, his leadership, his ability to attract the best talent, and other secrets to building the empire.

This book isn't just about Facebook, though the site is definitely an outstanding example of unprecedented success. I provide examples of multiple successful companies like Threadless, CollegeHumor, TOMS, Dyson, Zappos, and others to highlight the importance of every principle discussed in this book. Each of these companies has had amazing success in various industries and has thrived, I believe, due to values and principles similar to those discussed in this book.

But first, let's talk about you, the reader, and why this book is for you, no matter what your passions are.

Let's start with that bold word—entrepreneur!

To a handful of people, it is an exciting title, full of heavenly opportunities, audacious risk-taking, original ideas, and, of course, hard work. Entrepreneurs are the true darlings of the business culture. For the rest of us, this title seems, well, unattainable. While onstage, I once asked a corporate audience of about 600 people how many considered themselves "entrepreneurs," and only about 20 raised their hands. That's 3 percent.

Our understanding of entrepreneurship is flawed. We associate entrepreneurship with starting your own business, coming up with a completely new idea, and working in poverty in your garage 24/7 until you (maybe) hit it big. But that picture is not complete.

I bet most of the 600 people in that room either were already entrepreneurs or already had the makings of one; they just didn't know it. I bet there were many more than 20 people in that room who in their career took daring risks, challenged the status quo, came up with breakthrough ideas, and worked long hours to help their company (even if it wasn't founded by them) soar to new heights.

Those are *intrapreneurs*. David Armano, a friend and executive vice president at Edelman Digital, a global social agency, published a piece in *Forbes* in May 2012 titled "Move over Entrepreneurs, Here Come the Intrapreneurs." In the piece, he defined an intrapreneur as "someone who has an entrepreneurial streak in his or her DNA, but chooses to align his or her talents with a large organization in place of creating his or her own."[44] He argues that those individuals, when empowered by management, have the ability to innovate and produce true impact within any organization (small or large) at a similar scale of success as some entrepreneurs.

Scott Monty is an example of an intrapreneur. Global head of social media at Ford Motor Company, Scott helped fundamentally change the way the company engages with its customers online over the past four years. Says Scott:

> At Ford, we're still executing Henry Ford's original vision—"Opening the highways to all mankind." When you consider Henry Ford's entre-

preneurial spirit and vision, it should be clear why Ford was able to become a leader in the automotive world very quickly. The world has changed since Henry's time, but the spirit of risk taking, pushing ahead with a better plan, and sharing what we've learned for the advancement of the business world are all things that fuel us at Ford Motor Company. I count myself extremely fortunate to have been in a position to help the company continue to improve and adapt to the world around us and to make us more nimble and forward-thinking than many would have given us credit for.

Often it seems that entrepreneurs (or intrapreneurs) are single visionaries or lone wolves who get things done. At Ford, nothing could be further from the truth. Our "One Ford" mission means that we need to work together to accomplish our goals, and intrapreneurship follows these same principles. If a leader has a vision for what is possible, helps others to see the vision, and clearly communicates the expected outcome, it becomes easier to put it into practice.

Organizations small and large need intrapreneurs. In an era of constant change, not one single company can afford complacency. True disruption happens when entrepreneurial spirit is alive and well within an organization. And that spirit is cultivated and spread by intrapreneurs—those on the forefront of change, those passionate enough to activate the principles discussed in this book within their own organizations.

The thing is, you can be that person! Entrepreneur or intrapreneur, independent of our position within a company, I believe every single one of us can be a trailblazer if we are passionate enough and determined enough to stick to our vision and truly desire to change the world (even if in a small way).

The principles in this book are meant to help you learn from the most successful companies as you carve your own path to being an entrepreneur/intrapreneur.

So what is the book about?

In the following pages, I will look at five simple secrets that have the capacity to transform the not so simple world—the kind of transformation exemplified by Facebook. Each of five chapters explores a value or area of focus that I believe every successful start-up or organization possesses. All five values are embodied by Mark Zuckerberg as well as the founders of other companies mentioned in the book.

After working with start-ups for years, I know, of course, that there are more than five factors that influence the success of a venture. There is marketplace readiness and need, multiple environmental factors, resources, excellence of your product, appropriate partners, and the list goes on (including a little bit of luck).

When I was looking at the elements that made Facebook successful, a graphic emerged. I call it "Entrepreneurial Vision." It lists all of the major elements that influence the success of any venture. I drew it in a shape of an eye because I believe that any creation starts with looking at the world through your own unique lens, which shapes your specific vision. People

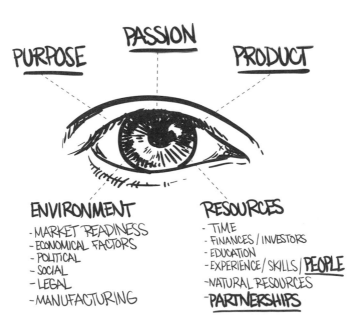

see the world of opportunities around them through the prism of their own experiences, their own passions. Those experiences and passions, in turn, shape the purpose of one's life. We all want to leave our own unique footprint in the world. And we do that through creating something of value, something that helps enrich people's lives. Like my father says: "Don't try to change the world. Find your purpose, live out your potential to the fullest, serve others kindly, and the world will change around you."

All great achievements start with *passion*. Passion is what fuels everything. Passion is what motivates you, whether your motivations are spiritual, artistic, political, economic, social, or personal. You know that you are passionate about something when you become restless, when you wake up every morning knowing that you cannot not create (or do) whatever it is that you are passionate about.

Passion is what shapes your *purpose*, in life and in business. When the idea for a venture starts taking shape, purpose is what ultimately helps define it. If you rally around the purpose and build a culture around it, you will meet success; if you lose your way, you will meet failure.

The successful execution of an idea or the realization of your purpose will depend on the current environment and a number of external factors, what I call *environment* in my graphic. A favorable environment is critical to a business's success. It includes factors such as readiness of the market to accept an idea or need; economic, political, and social factors; legal limitations; manufacturing capabilities; the personal situation of a founder; and many others. The problem with environmental factors is that most of the time, an entrepreneur cannot control them. So, even though she needs to consider them, she should focus instead on the factors she can control.

One such controllable factor is the entrepreneur's *product* or service. A well-designed product (or well-delivered service) is critical to the success of any endeavor. No one can be successful without a great product.

And last but not least, to grow any business, you need *resources*, which function as instruments of execution of your vision and creation of your product. Important resources could include time, capital, financing, education, experience, skills, people (employees), natural and/or manufacturing resources, investors, partners, and so forth. Even though all of these resources are important, I believe two impact the success of your company like no others: people and partnerships. Having the right (or wrong) people on board can make (or break) the success of a venture. And aligning with the right partners is a critical decision that may not always be the easiest to make.

It isn't my intention, however, to cover every single one of these elements in this book. We won't discuss environment, because obviously the marketplace was ready for Facebook. People had the need to connect online, broadband Internet penetration was on the rise, and the social digital era was starting to blossom, as evidenced by the popularity of companies such as Friendster and MySpace that were already starting to take off a year or so before Mark created Facebook. And we won't go into much detail on every single resource; Zuck obviously had the education, the skills, and time to work on his start-up. Rather, I would like to focus on two imperative resources that—in conjunction with passion, purpose, and product—helped him grow his vision into a global giant: hiring the right people and working with the right partners.

To me, there are five key principles, the five *P*s, that I believe were essential to Facebook's success and, as such, require a more in-depth look:

1. Passion

2. Purpose

3. People

4. Product

5. Partnerships

We'll explore each of these in more detail in the following chapters.

As I was writing this book, my mind kept wandering back to the graphic. It seemed that a fitting name for it would be "the EYE" ("Engaging

Your [Inner] Entrepreneur"), as I firmly believe that anyone can create something beautiful and meaningful if she looks within herself and finds something she is truly passionate about. Like Mark Zuckerberg did when he created Facebook. Let's talk about passion.

CHAPTER 1

PASSION

Find that thing you are super passionate about.
A lot of founding principles of Facebook are that if people
have access to more information and are more connected,
it will make the world better; people will have more
understanding, more empathy. That's the guiding
principle for me. On hard days, I really just step back,
and that's the thing that keeps me going.
—Mark Zuckerberg's advice to young entrepreneurs
in his March 25, 2011, appearance
at Brigham Young University in Utah[1]

People call him "The new Internet prince."

Zuckerberg does have some imperial tendencies. When he was a boy, he favored Civilization, a video game in which the object is to build an empire that will stand the test of time. Some of his friends are convinced that it served as a valuable exercise to prepare him to run his company.[2] A fencer in high school (a captain of the team, no less), Mark sometimes perceived the world as a fencing match, trying to build the right strategy and figure out the next move. Sometimes, he would pick up his foil and walk around with it, thinking out loud, delivering sudden thrusts here and there. Mark can read and write French, Hebrew, Latin, and ancient Greek (or so it said on his college application). In college, he was known for reciting lines from epic poems such as *The Iliad*. And in the early days of Facebook, you could hear the word *dominate* thrown around often in conversations among the boys. Zuck's dominance was indisputable. In the early days, a tagline accompanied every page of Facebook that read "A Mark Zuckerberg production," and on the About page, he was listed as "Founder, Master and Commander, Enemy of the State."[3] Given his knowledge of Latin, one can just imagine him proclaiming when reaching one billion users, "Veni, vidi, vici!" ("I came, I saw, I conquered") just as Julius Caesar reportedly said when celebrating a victory in 47 BC.

Zuck's confidence is oftentimes interpreted as arrogance. His direct stare can be unnerving. His tendency to tune out if he isn't interested in a conversation is well publicized. But isn't that what a man on a mission would do?

From an early age, Zuck was smitten with the intersection of software and social connections. At Harvard, he studied psychology and computer science. He created multiple little programs that explored the ways people connect with each other online, and he learned something new with each one of them. He wanted to bring the ways we communicate offline to the exploding world of online interactions. It became his passion. His passion powered his confidence. Says Ellen McGirt, a writer for *Fast Company*, in one of her stories about Zuck: "But he's not arrogant—he's profoundly certain."[4]

Mark got the technology bug from his father, Edward Zuckerberg. A dentist by profession, Ed had an admiration for technology. He bought every early computer he could. His very first purchase was in 1978, a personal computer called the Atari 800 that was designed for the casual computing enthusiast. That was the computer Mark learned to code on. Shortly thereafter, the Zuckerbergs purchased IBM's XT, which was installed in Ed's home office. Ed wasn't afraid to dabble in technology and learned how to code himself. Mark loved playing with machines as much as, if not more than, his father did. Ed cheered him on as well as his other kids: "You have to encourage them to pursue their passions."[5]

One of Zuck's first social coding experiments took place in the mid-nineties when his father got tired of hearing shouting from one room of his home dental practice to another announcing the arrival of a new patient. He wanted a more efficient approach. That's when Mark built a messaging system he called "Zucknet," which allowed one computer in the house to message another. The system was popular beyond Ed's office: Zuck and his three sisters, Randi, Donna, and Arielle, all used Zucknet to communicate with each other while working on their own computers in their rooms. The program he built was a simpler version of AOL's Instant Messenger, which came out the next year.

Mark enjoyed developing computer programs, especially ones that gave people the ability to interact with each other. He would code into the wee hours of the night. His Harvard friends recall a T-shirt he wore often: it pictured a little ape with the words "Code Monkey." In high school and during his first year of college, Mark built several smaller programs, including Synapse, CourseMatch, and Facemash. You could say Facemash was the reason he built Facebook. But more on that later.

Synapse Media Player, the program Zuck co-built in his senior year at Phillips Exeter Academy, used artificial intelligence to learn a listener's habits so that it could suggest other songs that matched what the user liked.

The program caught the attention of both Microsoft and AOL. They tried to recruit Mark, but he chose to attend Harvard instead.

Zuck created CourseMatch during his first week in college. The idea was to help students identify who took which classes on campus. Whether you wanted to hook up with a hot girl or hang out with the "cool" crowd, the program appealed to the status-conscious students at Harvard. It was also extremely useful in helping students form study groups for particular classes. As David Kirkpatrick notes in his book, *The Facebook Effect*, Zuck had created a program students wanted to use.

Encouraged by the success of CourseMatch, Mark couldn't wait to try out new ideas. The next month, he created Facemash, a program aimed at finding out who was the hottest person on campus. In a bold move, he invited users to compare two different faces of the same sex and vote for the hotter one. The project, completed in an eight-hour stretch, became an instant hit. People couldn't stop using it.

That is when the trouble started. Harvard turned off Mark's Internet access, and he was called before Harvard's disciplinary administrative board (along with the other two students who helped create Facemash). The problem was that he had hacked into the university system to obtain names and photos of the "participants" without permission from the university or students. He was able to get information on students from nine of Harvard's twelve houses (either through hacking in or getting a log-in from his friends). Harvard decided his actions constituted an inappropriate and unauthorized use of personal information. He was put on probation and asked to see a counselor. Before the site was shut down, students voted on 22,000 pairs of photos.[6]

The success of these experiments clearly showed Zuck that he had a knack for creating simple and addictive software. He also had passion. To connect people. To create an open world. It didn't matter in what format or for what purpose; Mark Zuckerberg had a strong desire to help people connect and, through that, to enrich their lives. He wanted to build a "social utility." At one time on his personal Facebook page, Zuck listed his personal interests as "openness, making things that help people connect and share what's important to them, revolutions, information flow, minimalism."[7] Today, the "About Mark" space on Zuck's page simply states: "I'm trying to make the world a more open place."

That passion is what helped him move on from the "failure" of Facemash toward the creation of Facebook. Except he didn't consider Facemash a failure. He considered it a monumental success. For one, it proved to him that there is a huge need for young people to bring their offline connections online. This stunt also came at a time when students were asking their universities to develop a site that would include key information about each student to facilitate easier connections on campus. He learned a lot from his experience. And those lessons, I believe, were critical to the success of Facebook's design and its early features.

When Facebook launched early the following year, Mark ensured that the sign-up was voluntarily and that students had the power to decide if they wanted to share any information with others. Students had to opt-in in order to participate and had the freedom to identify what types of information they wanted their friends to see. No hacking into systems or borrowing others' log-ins this time.

Lesson here? An experience such as the one Mark had with Facemash could be either a failure or a learning experience, depending on how you decide to look at it. If you are passionate about something, you most probably consider such an experience a valuable lesson and will apply it toward the next iteration of your idea. If you truly believe in something, nothing will stand in the way of making your idea a reality. Passion is a thin line between success and failure.

> There is no such thing as "failure" if you
> really want to pursue your dream.

False starts are simply invaluable learning experiences toward
the next iteration of an idea or a product.

That's the core philosophy behind the "hacker way": your product is never final; your work is never done. "For us," says Pedram Keyani, engineering manager of Facebook's site integrity team, "hacking is about passionately working toward a goal and not being afraid of failure."[8] Zuck has real vision, and he wants to see that vision executed. That is the reason he has never let go of his control of the company, even after its IPO. Some might call it "being a control freak," but I regard it as sheer brilliance on his part. "So many businesses get worried about looking like they might make a mistake, they become afraid to take any risk," Zuckerberg says with conviction. "Companies are set up so that people judge each other on failure. I am not going to get fired if we have a bad year. Or a bad five years. I don't have to worry about making things look good if they're not. I can actually set up the company to create value."[9] Creating value (even if you make a bunch of mistakes in the process) trumps everything else.

There is another lesson in Zuck's experiment with Facemash: perseverance. Mark heard the pleas of students and decided that if the university wouldn't provide something that students were asking for, he would be the one to build it for them. And, knowing Mark, he probably vowed to do it better than the university would anyway. He knew that after his stunt with Facemash, students worried that Harvard would reject similar projects altogether. He wasn't about to sit on sidelines and watch that happen. Hence, along came Facebook.

What I noticed is this: the most successful entrepreneurs always have one trait in common: they never give up. They know what they have to do, and there isn't a lot that can stop them. They fall, they get up, they move on. You move on because you have a goal, you have passion, and you have purpose. They cannot not do it! People with passion, propelled by their purpose, don't wait for the sunshine; they find the storm and ride it. In the words of Steve Jobs (during his 1995 interview with the Smithsonian Institute): "I'm convinced that about half of what separates the successful entrepreneurs from the non-successful ones is pure perseverance."[10]

Passion fuels perseverance—one of the key ingredients of success.

Interestingly enough, we have this misconception that our entrepreneurial ideas or the products we want to create have to be one hundred percent original, never done before. The truth is that some of the most successful entrepreneurs (as well as marketers, I might add) steal with pride. But what they do is make the final product original in all of the critical aspects, those that are truly important to both the creator and the consumer, which, in turn, makes it valuable.

That's exactly what Mark Zuckerberg did with Facebook.

What was the inspiration behind his success? How did he come up with the idea? His academic history offers much insight into his rise to fame. The concept might have been born when Zuck was still a student at Exeter, a private boarding school where he spent 2000–2002. The year Mark enrolled in school, he received his copy of the student directory called "The Photo Address Book." Students nicknamed the directory none other than "The Facebook." These books were essential to students' lives. Because Exeter students were not allowed cell phones on campus and they changed houses and phone numbers annually, the only way to keep up with friends was through those annually published books. Not only that, they found information such as where their peers resided, who was popular and who wasn't, who the new kids on campus were, and more. By the time Mark graduated and left school, Exeter's IT department was successful in placing the full directory online with the URL http://student.exeter.edu/

facebook.[11] The URL is no longer active, and Mark never officially commented on a story about the extent to which Exeter's Photo Address Book influenced him, but it's obvious that he saw a need that he could fill on college or high-school campuses that would help promote his life's goal of a connected world.

Harvard produced a similar annual book called the Freshman Register, which listed only entering students. Nevertheless, the books were extensively used. But the students wanted to have the ability to maintain their own information online. David Kirkpatrick writes in *The Facebook Effect*: "That fall Zuckerberg took a math class on graph theory. At semester's end everyone in the class went out to dinner and ended up talking about the need for a 'universal facebook.'"[12] Moreover, Zuck admitted to Kirkpatrick that Harvard's newsletter that covered the failure of Facemash gave him the initial idea of improving upon his experiment with Facemash. The newsletter wrote: "Much of the trouble surrounding the Facemash could have been eliminated if only the site had limited itself to students who voluntarily uploaded their own photos."[13]

Both of Facebook's competitors, MySpace and Friendster, were also launched the year before Zuck started Facebook. Friendster was primarily created to help people look for life partners, and people used it mostly for dating versus casual everyday connections. MySpace was a little bit more glamorous; it was open to anyone and allowed you to create a profile with either a real name or a pseudonym (which appealed to the entertainment industry).

Lesson here? The savvy entrepreneur is not afraid to use an inspiration that comes his way and sometimes steals with pride. Some of the most successful people see a need or identify a gap, and, if they are passionate enough, they help bridge it. They see the opportunity to do something better and go for it. But they do it in an original way, utilizing the knowledge and experience they have, as well as their beliefs. That is where passion plays a critical role. Your passion and purpose in life will manifest themselves in anything you create and in how you create it. For Zuckerberg, it was in building a "social graph" that held people responsible for presenting their true identities and giving them control over how much information they shared and how much of that information their friends saw. This was quite different from how his competitors approached their products.

James R. "Jim" Jarmusch, an American independent film director, screenwriter, and actor, said:

> Nothing is original. Steal from anywhere that resonates with inspiration or fuels your imagination. Devour old films, new films, music, books, paintings, photographs, poems, dreams, random conversations, architecture, bridges, street signs, trees, clouds, bodies of water, light and shadows. Select only things to steal from that speak directly to your soul. If you do this, your work (and theft) will be authentic. Authenticity is invaluable; originality is nonexistent. And don't bother concealing your thievery—celebrate it if you feel like it. In any case, always remember what Jean-Luc Godard said: "It's not where you take things from—it's where you take them to."[14]

It doesn't matter where inspiration comes from. Your idea may not be fully original, but always create your masterpiece authentically and with purpose.

Though at first sight the social network wasn't that different from its competitors MySpace and Friendster, Facebook was, in fact, quite unlike either. And that was due to Mark's beliefs.

Zuckerberg believes that the world is moving toward radical transparency. "Radical" is right. To Zuck, the information flow online shouldn't be encumbered by, well, anything. He believes the online world should be as much as possible a copy of the offline world. If you are talking to your friends, they know what you look like, they know your real name, they know what you like and don't like. Unlike other social networks of his time, Zuck wasn't interested in building a phony tool for phony profiles. He was extremely focused on ensuring that the social graph he helped create online would be transparent and authentic. Authenticity is everything to him. You are who you are, you have one identity, you are not two or three different people, and to him it is dishonest if you present anything other than your true self to the people around you. He believes in honesty of online self-expression just like in real life. Hence, Facebook's restriction of allowing only one profile per person. Believe it or not, people have been banned for creating multiple profiles.

Moreover, Zuck believes that the Internet will bring people together across the world. He is right—it already has. He believes there should be no borders, no restrictions, no limitations on not only the way people connect and communicate online but in the way information is created, consumed, and shared. There should be no secrets, only information and utilities that help enrich people's lives. He believes such tools and networks should be free. In creating Facebook, he used free open-source software like the MySQL database and Apache web server tools, which contributed to Facebook's success without requiring much financial backing up front. (Initially, Mark paid only for the hosting service and for the servers.)

Facebook was created on a principle of real-life identity and is intended to enhance your relationships with people you know in real life. One is not able to build trust inside online communities if one's identity isn't consistent and known to others. Facebook was the first social network to introduce this rule and demand compliance with it. From the beginning, the network also made sure to give users control of what information is shared and who sees their information. "Having two identities for yourself is an example of a lack of integrity," says Zuck.[15] Furthermore, he says, "The level of transparency the world has now won't support having two identities for a person."[16] He believes that such transparency will also help build a healthier society. He realizes that it is a challenge to get the world to the level of openness he would love to see, but he is confident that he is contributing to this cause by building Facebook and sticking to his goal consistently over the past eight years.

In contrast, MySpace wasn't very particular about who joined its network. Users could have multiple accounts and self-express in various ways under either a real name or a fake one. And you had full freedom to make your profile look any way you wanted. People also started to add friends like crazy; it became a competition for quantity over quality, as though the network wasn't created for personal connections but rather for popularity. MySpace was originally used by the entertainment and music industry. With the celebrities came their fans. Most of the time the behaviors, as well as the images shared on the site, were glamorous but risqué. For that reason, the site was considered "hip" and fun; anyone could pretend to be someone. Every image posted was carefully thought through; there weren't many casual photos taken on the go. The default setting was that everyone could see your account. By the time Facebook launched, MySpace was on its way to becoming the American social media darling with over one million users.

Facebook, however, was more of a social utility, a communication tool aimed at solving a very basic need—to keep track of your friends and converse with them casually. Its design was bland, and it didn't offer an option to upload multiple photos for a while (initially, users were restricted to only one photo). The site also authenticated your identity based on your college e-mail before it opened up to a wider audience. When Facebook introduced the feature that allowed users to upload multiple photos, people gravitated to the ability to take shots on the go when they were out and about with friends and began to share images of their kids, pets, favorite dishes, and much more without worrying about the quality or glamour of their lives, hence extending their "real life" online.

Throughout the existence of the social network, Zuck stuck to his passion and to the purpose of Facebook's creation. He always ensured that users came first and revenue second. Over the past eight years, he has been criticized for sacrificing revenue for users' interests. But he always sailed his course. "I never wanted to run a company," Zuckerberg said. "To me a business is a good vehicle for getting stuff done."[17] His belief in his company and its purpose was so strong, he declined to sell it over and over, even when Yahoo executives offered him $1 billion.

Money isn't a priority to him; he is more interested in building something genuinely amazing than selling out. For the longest time, he rented a small apartment and slept on a mattress on the floor. He drove an Acura TSX. He doesn't have fancy clothes, preferring T-shirts and hoodies. In the letter that accompanied the IPO, Zuck wrote: "Simply put: we don't build services to make money; we make money to build better services."[18] In that he reminds me of Steve Jobs and his quote from a 1993 *Wall Street Journal* interview: "Being the richest man in the cemetery doesn't matter to me. Going to bed at night saying we've done something wonderful, that's what matters to me."[19]

Zuckerberg also practices what he preaches. In a December 11, 2009, Facebook post on his personal page Mark wrote: "For those wondering, I set most of my content to be open so people could see it. I set some of my content to be more private, but I didn't see a need to limit visibility of pics with my friends, family or my teddy bear :)"

Even though money isn't a priority, Mark does care about the growth of the company and its monetization. But his primary focus is on "building something that actually makes a really big change in the world." He says: "The question I ask myself like almost every day is, 'Am I doing the most important thing I could be doing?' . . . Unless I feel like I'm working on the most important problem that I can help with, then I'm not going to feel good about how I'm spending my time. And that's what this company is."[20]

Zuck's business interests always aligned closely with his personal philosophy. He even encourages his employees to work on the projects they are passionate about, not the ones that are forcefully assigned to them. What an incredible way to take advantage of not only human competence, but full human potential.

We'll come back to the discussion of purpose, product, and people in the following chapters.

> Build what you believe in.
> Align your business interests with your personal philosophy.

I always have had enormous respect for entrepreneurs who are willing to stay the course and see their passion through, no matter what criticism, such as Estée Lauder, Amelia Earhart, Steve Jobs, Warren Buffett, Oprah Winfrey, Jeff Bezos, Bill Gates, Mary Kay Ash, Coco Chanel, Madame C. J. Walker, Jack Welch, Mark Zuckerberg, and many other lesser-known names. "A big piece of the story we tell ourselves about who we are is that we are willing to invent," said Amazon CEO Jeff Bezos. "And, very importantly, we are willing to be misunderstood for long periods of time."[21] Zuck seems to agree—he doesn't seek approval, he has his passion and his vision, and he is willing to sacrifice to execute on that vision.

Interesting thing, passion. When one does what one loves, she can move mountains. Studies and experience show that following your passions leads to great success.

In his book *Getting Rich Your Own Way,* Srully Blotnick, an American author and journalist, talks about a study done over 20 years (from 1960 to 1980) with 1,500 business school graduates, tracking their success after graduation based on their career choices. All 1,500 people were asked the same question: would you pursue your dream now or pursue a career that will help you become financially secure first? Eighty-three percent of people responded that they would wait until they were financially secure and then pursue their dreams. Seventeen percent opted to go for their dream now and think about money later.

Twenty years later, out of the 255 graduates who chose work they truly loved, 100 were millionaires. Out of the 1,245 graduates who decided to chase a bigger paycheck over what they were passionate about, only one ended up becoming a millionaire.[22]

Remarkable! What this study shows is that unless there is a strong drive attached to your future, unless there is some purpose attached to your dreams, it is very unlikely that they will come true. Why? In my humble opinion, Warren Buffett said it best: "Without passion, you don't have energy. Without energy, you have nothing."[23]

Passion fuels your success. No doubt. A number of extraordinary people have proven that. But I also want to focus on another trait shared by every great entrepreneur who achieved success: the ability to act! Without action, your desire is just that—a desire. No result can come out of a desire if you don't execute on it. That is what separates great entrepreneurs from good ones: they act, not plan. Estée Lauder once said: "I didn't get where I am by thinking about it or dreaming it. I got there by doing it."[24]

I would actually go so far as to say that one doesn't have to be a genius to create something extraordinary. Sometimes average people are the ones who spearhead true change. And that is because they are willing to act on their passion. They are willing to be wrong, to risk everything. They are willing to fail, get up, and try again. Passion serves as a catalyst to the execution of an idea. Those who are passionate enough to pioneer true change are those most likely to deliver on it.

I've worked with a lot of businesses throughout my career, from start-ups to major corporations. I've seen brilliant people come up with fantastic ideas. I've witnessed grandiose dreams and golden opportunities. And most of those just passed by because they weren't executed upon. And then I've watched average people with less authority, less resources, less education, and lack of needed experience create successful ventures because they were so dedicated to a dream or a goal that it was impossible for them to not create a masterpiece. I have also seen some of those ventures fail, but it wasn't for lack of trying. Those who continued to redefine themselves but stayed true to the same passions and the same key goals did succeed.

To be brutally honest, if you are an intrapreneur and you work within a big brand, it can be difficult to achieve the freedom to execute on those opportunities. You have to have strong faith and the support of your management to take the risks necessary and to get the essential resources. However, in a true spirit of innovation and entrepreneurship, I've also seen intrapreneurs execute without many resources, adopting an attitude of "take a risk now and ask for forgiveness later." Whether it is right or wrong, I can't judge—every situation is different. But I also know that you cannot challenge the status quo and you cannot truly disrupt if you don't take that step. Like Intel's beloved chief marketing officer, Deborah Conrad, says: "You are not truly disrupting if you are not making someone uncomfortable."

Mark Zuckerberg could have only talked about the social network of his dreams, like many of his peers at Exeter and many of the students at Harvard. But he was the only one who had the guts to take the plunge and act on it. He thought through it, he designed it, he came up with the features, he paid for the hosting company, and he launched it on an average night no different from any other when he played with the coding of his other projects.

In his interview with *Time* magazine in 2010, the year *Time* named him the Person of the Year, Zuck said, "The craziest thing to me in all this is that I remember having these conversations with my friends when I was in college. We would just sort of take it as an assumption that the world would get to the state where it is now. But, we figured, we're just college kids. Why were we the people who were most qualified to do that? I mean, that's crazy!

[pause] I guess what it probably turns out is, other people didn't care as much as we did."[25]

Doers always act! The word *possibilities* always translates for them as "possible it is!" To them, that's how a dream becomes a reality. A Facebook poster hung in the Palo Alto headquarters reads: "Done is better than perfect."

Passion + Action = Results

Mark cares about changing the lives of people around the world by giving them access to information and an ability to share it. To him, global transparency breeds global trust. It creates a fairer and better-governed world. It is the tool for promoting freedom and democracy. It is about giving an individual the same power that media has, about leveling the playing field. In his comments to the audience on his Spanish trip, he noted: "Making the world more open is not an overnight thing. It's a ten-to-fifteen-year thing." He is in it for the long haul. Peter Thiel, a venture capitalist and Zuck's friend, has fully bought into his vision:

> People in a globalized world are going to be in closer proximity to each other. The key value in my mind will be more tolerance. What I like about the Facebook model is it's centered on real human beings, and it enables them to become friends with other people and build relationships not only in the context they're already in but in contexts outside of that as well. Globalization doesn't necessarily mean you are friends with everybody in the world. But it somehow means that you're open to a lot more people in a lot more contexts than you would have been before.

Humans in their minds are more important than technology. "Helping the world's people self-organize is the most important thing," says Thiel.[26]

That is why Thiel invested in the network early on and now sits on Facebook's board of directors.

With anything you do, you always encounter criticism. And the bigger you are, the bigger the target on your back. Such is the case with Facebook. It is often criticized for its disregard for privacy in favor of this radical openness concept. It seems that the younger generation isn't as concerned with privacy issues as the older generation is. A lot of youngsters who were brought up in a global village welcome the openness and opportunities that Facebook provides them, such as being a platform for speaking up and seeking out like-minded people. I won't argue with the fact that privacy is a serious issue to consider always. But I also believe that it is a two-way street, that it is a matter of personal responsibility as well. I am of the opinion that one shouldn't share something one wouldn't be comfortable sharing with the whole world anywhere online. Everything we do online or offline is a personal choice. And so is our decision about what to share on social networks.

In doing research for this book, I found this post by Facebook's engineer, Michael Novati. It shows how much Facebook employees share Zuck's vision and, in this case, Michael's personal interpretation of "openness":

THOUGHTS ON "OPENNESS"

by **Michael Novati** on Wednesday, December 15, 2010 at 8:07 pm

As a loyal Facebook engineer and Facebook fan boy, I naturally support Facebook when it comes to its position on many debatable topics. The topic that comes up the most is by far Facebook's position on "openness." Facebook's mission is to empower people to share and make the world more open and connected, but we don't usually define what "open" means. This is the source of most debate I have with people about the topic.

Open is not meant to be taken personally. I don't think Facebook's mission is to make each and every person share private information and make it public for everyone to see.

Open is meant to be taken universally. Facebook wants the world as a whole to be more open and transparent. Looking back over the past hundreds of years, the printing press is a good analogy. The printing press allowed for information previously available only to a select few to be available to the masses, enabling everyone to make better and more informed choices. Another example is the Internet, which has given people access to more points of view and real-time information on almost anything that happens anywhere in the world. Facebook wants to play this kind of role in the world by helping you share with, and get information from, your friends and extended network.

So the message that I think you should take personally about Facebook's point of view on openness is to think about how Facebook has helped you make better decisions about things, and in return what you can do using Facebook to help others make better decisions about things. This last sentence is what often gets exaggerated into "Facebook wants me to share everything with everyone," but that's simply not the case.

Anyways, those are my random thoughts on openness written in 5 mins.

Thanks,

Michael[27]

"I know it sounds corny," Mark Zuckerberg said in an interview with *Stanford Daily*. "But I'd love to improve people's lives, especially socially."[28]

Passion ignites us, motivates us, and helps us persevere through many challenges. Zuck wasn't the only one driven by passion. A lot of great entrepreneurs have found that passion is one of the most crucial ingredients of their success.

Thirty-five-year-old Blake Mycoskie is one of them. TOMS is one of my favorite brands. I am not sure what I am drawn to more, TOMS Shoes' great comfort or the story behind the brand. An entrepreneur since college, Mycoskie started multiple businesses. But his most significant contribution to the world was spearheading the TOMS movement. I call it a "movement" because TOMS is more of a movement than a company. While vacationing in South America in 2006, Mycoskie was struck by the terrible poverty he saw. Children would walk around without shoes, developing cuts that resulted in injury and disease. He vowed that he would find a way to help. And he did. Blake's business concept is simple: for every pair of shoes he sells, the company donates one to a kid in need—one for one. Since the founding of TOMS about six years ago, thousands have joined Mycoskie's effort to supply shoes to kids living in poverty. The movement has touched children in over 40 countries. When he started his business, some called him crazy. "That kind of business model isn't possible!" they said. But Blake Mycoskie persisted. Because of his passion, perseverance, and can-do attitude, millions of children around the world (including many in the United States) have been given the gift of new shoes thanks to Blake and his "shoe drops."

Chris Gardner is another example of great success despite the odds. A multimillionaire stockbroker, investor, and philanthropist, he was once a young man struggling with homelessness while raising his toddler son, Christopher Jr. You might remember his story from his book and the movie *The Pursuit of Happyness*, starring Will Smith. Gardner once shared his secret to success: finding something you love to do so much, you can't wait for the sun to rise to do it all over again. He explains that the most inspiring leaders are not those who do their job, but those who pursue a calling.

And, of course, Steve Jobs believed in the power of passion. He once said, "People with passion can change the world for the better." Jobs claimed that the passion he had for his work made all the difference in his life. He gave this advice in his 2005 Stanford commencement address: "If you haven't found it yet, keep looking. Don't settle. As with all matters of the heart, you'll know when you find it. And, like any great relationship, it just gets better and better as the years roll on."[29]

Your passions help you understand who you are and what you want to do with your life. That understanding shapes your purpose. And purpose is what crafts your ideas, defines your creations, molds your products, and propels your innovation. Purpose is the heart of your business.

CHAPTER 2

PURPOSE

*Founded in 2004, Facebook's mission is to make
the world more open and connected. People use Facebook
to stay connected with friends and family,
to discover what's going on in the world, and to share
and express what matters to them.*

—About Facebook statement accompanying company's press releases

In the sixties, the number four was associated with the Beatles, who became an international sensation. But in 1960, the number four was linked to a different kind of story that drew worldwide attention—the survival tale of four Soviet soldiers. At the time, the story was so unusual, so inspiring, that a movie, *49 Days*, was made to celebrate the strength of the human spirit it portrayed.

On the night of January 17, 1960, during a hurricane, the ropes of a small self-propelled barge, anchored at one of the Kuril Islands, were torn off by the strong wind. The barge was carried away to one of the most turbulent areas of the Pacific Ocean. Four Soviet soldiers were on board: Master Sergeant Ashat Ziganschin, 21; Private Anatoliy Kruchkowsky, 22; Private Philipp Poplavski, 20; and Private Ivan Fedotov, 20.

The four men fought the ocean waves, struggling to get their boat back to shore. They tried to send a message to the base, but the radio was nonresponsive. After a while, the engine stopped. Soaking wet, shivering from the icy water, and dead tired from trying to keep the boat afloat, the men fought the raging storm for 50 long hours.

To make matters worse, the barge had only two days worth of emergency food rations. That, and two buckets of potatoes, didn't amount to much. The situation was beyond desperate. The four men didn't know how long they would have to survive in the open ocean, or if they would survive at all. Honoring the military vow of "no man left behind," they swore to support each other in their situation no matter what and do everything they could to work toward the same goal—getting all four of them home safely.

From the first day, they were compelled to ration their food and drink. They cooked soup (made out of one potato boiled in water) every other day. The five mouthfuls of fresh water they drank daily were collected from the occasional rain. On very rare occasions when the sea was calmer, they tried to fish with hooks made of nails. But no matter how hard they tried, they never caught a fish. By the end of February, all food supplies were gone. The soldiers started boiling leather straps and the soles of their shoes. They cut them into thin strips to make them easier to swallow.

Gradually, they became so weak they were not able to pump water out of the boat. They each lost 35 to 40 pounds. Their sight started to fail. But they stayed optimistic and united, never taking any food from one another and cheering each other up as much as they could. Between constant storms, they sang songs and played the accordion (until they had to cut it up for food). During their endless drift, they saw ships in the distance on three occasions. They signaled for help, but their boat was too small to spot.

On March 6, about 1,000 miles west-northwest of Midway Island, a U.S. Navy pilot spotted a tiny barge in the rough sea with four men on deck. He reported it to the commander of the aircraft carrier USS *Kearsarge*, who proceeded with an immediate rescue mission. When they were brought on board, the four men were coherent but extremely weakened. They had been adrift in the ocean for 49 days.[1]

For 49 days, the four men struggled to survive. With no means of communication and constant raging storms, they had no idea how long they would stay alive. Trying to keep the boat afloat every single day was no easy task. It was hard to constantly stay alert enough to ensure that the boat didn't run into the rocks or get flooded with water. Their hope should have slipped away with their limited supplies. But it didn't. Why? They were united by a single purpose, their motivation unwavering.

You see, the purpose that drives a strong mission can mobilize colossal physical and spiritual strength. That strength is the source of human miracles. The four Soviet soldiers offer an extreme example of the resilience of the human spirit in the toughest of conditions. But just as their goal of getting home safely helped them survive without losing a single teammate, any business with a clear purpose has the ability to not only survive turbulent times but to thrive long-term.

A business's purpose is its fundamental reason for being.

In his book *Start with Why*, Simon Sinek talks about the power of a core belief or a cause, of what he calls the "why." The *why* is the reason you get up every morning, the reason you (or your company) exist, the reason you do what you do every single day. "People don't buy WHAT you do, they buy WHY you do it," he insists throughout his book.[2]

Great leaders (and great companies) create movements, not just products. "Those [leaders] who are able to inspire give people a sense of purpose or belonging that has little to do with any external incentive or benefit to be gained," Simon Sinek writes. "Those who truly lead are able to create a following of people who act not because they are swayed, but because they were inspired. For those who are inspired, the motivation to act is deeply personal." Whether they have a desire to work with you toward a shared goal or to buy your product because your company stands for something they believe in, people want to matter. It is a basic human need to be around those who share our beliefs. The sense of one purpose, of belonging, of we-are-in-this-together is a feeling that inspires. Purpose is essential to the success of any endeavor. It gives organizations true authenticity.

> **Great companies don't just create great products,
> they create movements.**

Everything a successful company does stems from its purpose: the products it makes, the employees it hires, the working environment it creates, the customers and investors it attracts, the partnerships it forges, the way it markets its products or services, and the way it delivers customer service. The reality is that any new product or service can be copied, the quality can be made comparable, the incentives can be offered, and the prices can be cut in an effort to make a company competitive. But what really breeds long-term customer loyalty (and with it success of the company) isn't a specific product or a discount but rather the authentic belief your customers hold that binds them to your company and makes them relate to your company's mission in the world. That is what speaks to customers' emotions, dreams, and values.

Throughout his book, Sinek keeps coming back to Apple. The company offers an ideal example. Despite the odds, Apple remained successful under the vision of one of its founders, Steve Jobs. We look at Apple's higher pricing and smaller market share and wonder how it succeeded. One of the main reasons, Sinek believes, is that Apple was clear about the reason for its existence. The company's "Think Different" slogan inspired a generation and consistently encouraged people to challenge the status quo. The slogan also embodied Apple's choice to walk the path less traveled in creating every single one of its products. At the time Steve Jobs and Steve Wozniak were turning their passion into purpose and then into action, computers were considered business tools, not personal tools. The form factors and price points were such that a regular person couldn't afford one. Apple started with the passion of its founders—to get personal computers into the hands of every individual—which turned into the purpose of challenging the conventional wisdom and changing the world, one product at a time.

Apple's success was amazing. In its first year of existence, the company made a million dollars in revenue. In six years, it was a billion dollar company. And that is not only because Apple lives and breathes its purpose in everything it does; it is also because the company clearly communicates its beliefs to the world. Apple's people believe in the power of the individual and in empowering individuals to challenge the status quo, to create a revolution. And it is obvious in their every action. Like their marketing, for one. The "I'm a Mac. And I'm a PC." commercials struck a chord; people could relate to the confident and rebellious Mac guy making fun of the old, orthodox PC guy. The company introduced the iPod by offering people "1,000 songs in your pocket." Says Sinek: "Apple did not invent the mp3, nor did they invent the technology that became the iPod, yet they are credited with transforming the music industry with it."[3] That is because the company didn't market a product itself but rather marketed the reason why people wanted it. Products that represent a belief or a purpose allow people to indirectly communicate their sense of who they are and where they belong. Apple's founders, Apple's employees, Apple's customers—they all exist to push the envelope, to rebel against the conventional.

Making a positive impact in the world in one way or another seems to be the purpose of every successful business. Apple's belief—its purpose—hasn't changed since its inception. It has stayed consistent through its history. So has Ford's purpose of "opening the highways to all mankind"; Southwest Airlines' purpose to provide affordable transportation to the common person; Walt Disney's purpose to bring joy to children everywhere; Starbucks' purpose to bring people together, to "inspire and nurture the human spirit—one person, one cup, and one neighborhood at at time"; Zappos' purpose to delight its patrons through "wow" customer service; and Coca-Cola's purpose to inspire happiness. Just like the DNA in our bodies, purpose should be the core, the DNA, of a business. And every action of that business should authentically articulate its heritage.

Ignited by Mark Zuckerberg's passion, his Harvard friends got together numerous times to discuss the topic of changing the world. They talked about a better, more open, and empathetic world. From that, Facebook's purpose was born—"to make the world more open and connected." His friends, who shared Zuck's beliefs, rallied behind that purpose of building communication bridges between people, and they dropped out of college to help Zuck make it a reality. They set out to build a directory of people, a gateway to the people in our lives we care about. They wanted to bring our offline world online.

Now, with close to 4,000 employees, Facebook always buzzes with passion, excitement, focused activity, and sheer determination. Why? It isn't because Zuck is charismatic. He may be brilliant, but he isn't charismatic socially. But when he starts talking about Facebook and its mission, people cannot not pay attention. And Facebook employees will probably argue with me on the "Zuck isn't charismatic" point till their throats are sore. That is because they are true believers, because the whole company is united by the same mission.

Facebook's mission statement has evolved over the years together with the product. But it did so in wording, not in purpose. Here is its evolution:

- **2004:** "Facebook is an online directory that connects people through social networks at colleges."

- **2005:** "Facebook is an online directory that connects people through social networks at schools." (At that time, Facebook became available in high schools as well.)

- **2006–2007:** "Facebook is a social utility that connects you with the people around you."

- **2008:** "Facebook helps you connect and share with the people in your life."

- **2009:** "Facebook gives people the power to share and make the world more open and connected."[4]

- **2010–2011:** "Founded in February 2004, Facebook's mission is to give people the power to share and make the world more open and connected. Anyone can sign up for Facebook and interact with the people they know in a trusted environment."

- **2012:** "Founded in 2004, Facebook's mission is to make the world more open and connected. People use Facebook to stay connected with friends and family, to discover what's going on in the world, and to share and express what matters to them."

> A company's direction may change as it grows,
> but the true purpose of a successful company stays the same.

In the "now" economy of the Internet boom, it wasn't unusual for start-ups to be bought out once they became decent business prospects. That sort of instant gratification approach never sat well with Zuckerberg. He had a vision, and he was willing to pursue it tenaciously to the end. This doesn't mean he didn't have his doubts at times, but he saw Facebook's full potential and was against selling it. In 2004, when he was approached with a $10 million offer, he didn't even stop to consider it. During Viacom's 2005 courtship, Michael Wolf asked Zuck why he didn't want to sell; after all, he would become rather wealthy. "You just saw my apartment," Mark replied. "I don't really need any money." Even with the $2 billion valuation that was thrown around in their discussion, Wolf remembered Zuck's lack of interest during the conversation: "It wasn't like 'I want $2 billion.' It was, 'If you pay me $2 billion, I don't want to sell. Thank you.'" Next year, Zuck walked away from a $1 billion deal with Yahoo. His explanation for declining the offer was: "I can't really explain it. I just know."[5] For him, the journey wasn't complete yet; he knew he could take Facebook much further by not selling it, by staying the course and sticking to his purpose. He knew there was much more opportunity ahead to make an impact, to change the world.

"I'm here to build something for the long-term," Zuck says. "Anything else is a distraction."[6] It is important to him that people understand that what he is doing now is only the beginning. "The companies that succeed and have the best impact and are able to outcompete everyone else are the ones that have the longest time horizon," he states.[7] One of the most famous Facebook slogans is: "The journey is only 1% finished." Mark doesn't like it when people ask him, "What is your exit strategy?" He says he isn't building to sell, so he doesn't think about it. He builds to last.

Zuck always was, and continues to be, adamant about maintaining control of the company and its direction, even post-IPO (he owns 55.8 percent of voting shares). He understands that to enforce his long-term vision and to keep the company on the right path, he needs to be able to make tough decisions in the face of pressure from stakeholders and naysayers. He looks at examples of other companies that lost control post-IPO and eventually lost track of their vision, and he doesn't want to repeat their mistakes. He doesn't want the one-sided view of short-term investors to impact the future of the company. He is following the great example of Jeff Bezos and sticking to his guns. After Amazon went public in 1997, Bezos discounted those who said that his company wouldn't make money. And once he proved otherwise, he once again discounted those who complained that the company wasn't making enough money. In 2012, Amazon stock was trading way over 100 times its IPO price. The road wasn't always smooth; those investors who didn't believe in the company's vision did suffer losses from the sale of their stock after the tech bubble burst. Those who stuck with the company now enjoy a hefty profit. Zuckerberg knows that Facebook's stock price will probably follow the same ups and downs as Amazon's once did; no road to executing your long-term vision is ever easy or straight. But time and time again, successful companies have proven that long-term vision is something worth fighting for.

> Build your company with a long-term vision. Build it to last.
> And if you want to see your long-term vision come to life,
> try to maintain control as long as you possibly can.

Whenever anyone asks Zuck about his priorities, he always cites growth and constant improvement in user experience. From the beginning, he wanted to build a solid product first and then focus on revenue, as late as possible. It made it hard for those responsible for the operations side to work with him. Advertisers who brought in most of the company's revenue demanded flexibility and bigger space on the site, but Zuck refused every single time. He was adamant about preserving the user experience. His decree was that advertising should be useful for the user no matter what. He felt it was wrong to make money off of advertising if it wasn't adding value. He said no to anything that interfered with the ease of use and fluidity of the site. He gets frustrated by constant comments about money over the mission. He says: "One thing that is personally a bit disheartening. . . . It bums me out that people immediately go to 'You must be doing this to make money.' Because that's just so different from the ethos of the company. It is so different from how we actually think about stuff that you feel so misunderstood."[8] In his IPO letter, he states: "Simply put: we don't build services to make money; we make money to build better services."

The letter that Zuckerberg included in Facebook's IPO prospectus is very direct about his priorities for the company. According to *New York* magazine, he wrote the letter himself because it was important to him that "everyone who invests in Facebook understands what this mission means to us [at Facebook], how we make decisions, and why we do the things we do." The letter is worth a close read, because it clearly shows Zuck's passion, the company's purpose for existence, his long-term vision, and the company's five values:

- Focus on impact

- Be fast

- Be bold

- Be open

- Build social value

Here's the full text of the letter:[9]

Facebook was not originally created to be a company. It was built to accomplish a social mission—to make the world more open and connected.

We think it's important that everyone who invests in Facebook understands what this mission means to us, how we make decisions and why we do the things we do. I will try to outline our approach in this letter.

At Facebook, we're inspired by technologies that have revolution-ized how people spread and consume information. We often talk about inventions like the printing press and the television—by simply making communication more efficient, they led to a complete transformation of many important parts of society. They gave more people a voice. They encouraged progress. They changed the way society was organized. They brought us closer together.

Today, our society has reached another tipping point. We live at a moment when the majority of people in the world have access to the internet or mobile phones—the raw tools necessary to start shar-ing what they're thinking, feeling and doing with whomever they want. Facebook aspires to build the services that give people the power to share and help them once again transform many of our core institutions and industries.

There is a huge need and a huge opportunity to get everyone in the world connected, to give everyone a voice and to help transform soci-ety for the future. The scale of the technology and infrastructure that must be built is unprecedented, and we believe this is the most impor-tant problem we can focus on.

We hope to strengthen how people relate to each other.

Even if our mission sounds big, it starts small—with the relationship between two people.

Personal relationships are the fundamental unit of our society. Relationships are how we discover new ideas, understand our world and ultimately derive long-term happiness.

At Facebook, we build tools to help people connect with the peo-ple they want and share what they want, and by doing this we are extending people's capacity to build and maintain relationships.

People sharing more—even if just with their close friends or fami-lies—creates a more open culture and leads to a better understanding of the lives and perspectives of others. We believe that this creates a greater number of stronger relationships between people, and that it helps people get exposed to a greater number of diverse perspectives.

By helping people form these connections, we hope to rewire the way people spread and consume information. We think the world's information infrastructure should resemble the social graph—a network built from the bottom up or peer-to-peer, rather than the monolithic, top-down structure that has existed to date. We also believe that giving people control over what they share is a fundamental principle of this rewiring.

We have already helped more than 800 million people map out more than 100 billion connections so far, and our goal is to help this rewiring accelerate.

We hope to improve how people connect to businesses and the economy.

We think a more open and connected world will help create a stronger economy with more authentic businesses that build better products and services.

As people share more, they have access to more opinions from the people they trust about the products and services they use. This makes it easier to discover the best products and improve the quality and efficiency of their lives.

One result of making it easier to find better products is that businesses will be rewarded for building better products—ones that are personalized and designed around people. We have found that products that are "social by design" tend to be more engaging than their traditional counterparts, and we look forward to seeing more of the world's products move in this direction.

Our developer platform has already enabled hundreds of thousands of businesses to build higher-quality and more social products. We have seen disruptive new approaches in industries like games, music and news, and we expect to see similar disruption in more industries by new approaches that are social by design.

In addition to building better products, a more open world will also encourage businesses to engage with their customers directly and authentically. More than four million businesses have Pages on Facebook that they use to have a dialogue with their customers. We expect this trend to grow as well.

We hope to change how people relate to their governments and social institutions.

We believe building tools to help people share can bring a more honest and transparent dialogue around government that could lead to more direct empowerment of people, more accountability for officials and better solutions to some of the biggest problems of our time.

By giving people the power to share, we are starting to see people make their voices heard on a different scale from what has historically been possible. These voices will increase in number and volume. They cannot be ignored. Over time, we expect governments will become more responsive to issues and concerns raised directly by all their people rather than through intermediaries controlled by a select few.

Through this process, we believe that leaders will emerge across all countries who are pro-internet and fight for the rights of their people, including the right to share what they want and the right to access all information that people want to share with them.

Finally, as more of the economy moves towards higher-quality products that are personalized, we also expect to see the emergence of new services that are social by design to address the large worldwide problems we face in job creation, education and health care. We look forward to doing what we can to help this progress.

OUR MISSION AND OUR BUSINESS

As I said above, Facebook was not originally founded to be a company. We've always cared primarily about our social mission, the services we're building and the people who use them. This is a different approach for a public company to take, so I want to explain why I think it works.

I started off by writing the first version of Facebook myself because it was something I wanted to exist. Since then, most of the ideas and code that have gone into Facebook have come from the great people we've attracted to our team.

Most great people care primarily about building and being a part of great things, but they also want to make money. Through the process of building a team—and also building a developer community, advertising market and investor base—I've developed a deep appreciation for how building a strong company with a strong economic engine and strong growth can be the best way to align many people to solve important problems.

Simply put: we don't build services to make money; we make money to build better services.

And we think this is a good way to build something. These days I think more and more people want to use services from companies that believe in something beyond simply maximizing profits.

By focusing on our mission and building great services, we believe we will create the most value for our shareholders and partners over the long term—and this in turn will enable us to keep attracting the best people and building more great services. We don't wake up in the morning with the primary goal of making money, but we understand that the best way to achieve our mission is to build a strong and valuable company.

This is how we think about our IPO as well. We're going public for our employees and our investors. We made a commitment to them when we gave them equity that we'd work hard to make it worth a lot and make it liquid, and this IPO is fulfilling our commitment. As we become a public company, we're making a similar commitment to our new investors and we will work just as hard to fulfill it.

THE HACKER WAY

As part of building a strong company, we work hard at making Facebook the best place for great people to have a big impact on the world and learn from other great people. We have cultivated a unique culture and management approach that we call the Hacker Way.

The word "hacker" has an unfairly negative connotation from being portrayed in the media as people who break into computers. In reality, hacking just means building something quickly or testing the boundaries of what can be done. Like most things, it can be used for good or bad, but the vast majority of hackers I've met tend to be idealistic people who want to have a positive impact on the world.

The Hacker Way is an approach to building that involves continuous improvement and iteration. Hackers believe that something can always be better, and that nothing is ever complete. They just have to go fix it—often in the face of people who say it's impossible or are content with the status quo.

Hackers try to build the best services over the long term by quickly releasing and learning from smaller iterations rather than trying to get everything right all at once. To support this, we have built a testing framework that at any given time can try out thousands of versions of Facebook. We have the words "Done is better than perfect" painted on our walls to remind ourselves to always keep shipping.

Hacking is also an inherently hands-on and active discipline. Instead of debating for days whether a new idea is possible or what the best way to build something is, hackers would rather just prototype something and see what works. There's a hacker mantra that you'll hear a lot around Facebook offices: "Code wins arguments."

Hacker culture is also extremely open and meritocratic. Hackers believe that the best idea and implementation should always win—not the person who is best at lobbying for an idea or the person who manages the most people.

To encourage this approach, every few months we have a hackathon, where everyone builds prototypes for new ideas they have. At the end, the whole team gets together and looks at everything that has been built. Many of our most successful products came out of hackathons, including Timeline, chat, video, our mobile development framework and some of our most important infrastructure like the HipHop compiler.

To make sure all our engineers share this approach, we require all new engineers—even managers whose primary job will not be to write code—to go through a program called Bootcamp where they learn our codebase, our tools and our approach. There are a lot of folks in the industry who manage engineers and don't want to code themselves, but the type of hands-on people we're looking for are willing and able to go through Bootcamp.

The examples above all relate to engineering, but we have distilled these principles into *five core values for how we run Facebook*:

Focus on Impact

If we want to have the biggest impact, the best way to do this is to make sure we always focus on solving the most important problems. It sounds simple, but we think most companies do this poorly and waste a lot of time. We expect everyone at Facebook to be good at finding the biggest problems to work on.

Move Fast

Moving fast enables us to build more things and learn faster. However, as most companies grow, they slow down too much because they're more afraid of making mistakes than they are of losing opportunities by moving too slowly. We have a saying: "Move fast and break things." The idea is that if you never break anything, you're probably not moving fast enough.

Be Bold

Building great things means taking risks. This can be scary and prevents most companies from doing the bold things they should. However, in a world that's changing so quickly, you're guaranteed to fail if you don't take any risks. We have another saying: "The riskiest thing is to take no risks." We encourage everyone to make bold decisions, even if that means being wrong some of the time.

Be Open

We believe that a more open world is a better world because people with more information can make better decisions and have a greater impact. That goes for running our company as well. We work hard to make sure everyone at Facebook has access to as much information as possible about every part of the company so they can make the best decisions and have the greatest impact.

Build Social Value

Once again, Facebook exists to make the world more open and connected, and not just to build a company. We expect everyone at Facebook to focus every day on how to build real value for the world in everything they do.

Thanks for taking the time to read this letter. We believe that we have an opportunity to have an important impact on the world and build a lasting company in the process. I look forward to building something great together.

Zuck's belief in openness and connectedness is also built into Facebook's culture. Hacker culture is at the core of Facebook. It is a culture of deep collaboration, constant agility, and desire to improve the current product. "What most people think when they hear the word 'hacker' is breaking into things," Zuck said. To Facebook's founder, hacker culture is a group's ability to build something better than one individual could: "There's an intense focus on openness, sharing information, as both an ideal and a practical strategy to get things done."[10] Zuckerberg gives engineers full freedom—everyone can contribute, every suggestion counts. His word is final, though; he ensures that everything the company does (including countless product iterations) is in line with his vision.

Mark's critics think his view of openness is too naive. He is young and inexperienced, they say. He doesn't fully grasp the importance of privacy and other important issues. But Mark believes he does. "We realize that people will probably criticize us for this for a long time, but we just believe that this is the right thing to do," he said in a 2010 interview with *The New Yorker*.

"If you go back 10 years, a lot of people were afraid of sharing things on the Internet," Zuckerberg once said. "One of the things that initially got people comfortable is that we offer extremely robust privacy controls. A lot of folks now understand they know where their information is going . . . We're really focusing on safety, especially children's safety . . . We really try to build a safe environment."[11]

That is true. Facebook puts great focus on security. They continuously work on simplifying privacy controls and coming up with new innovations to protect user information. As I was writing this chapter while visiting my parents in Europe, I accessed the Internet through an unfamiliar Wi-Fi. When I logged into Facebook, the site detected the change and asked me to verify my information. It gave me a choice: ask a personal security question or show me pictures of my friends to match their photos with their identity. I chose the latter. As I was going through the pictures of four or five of my friends, I took my time to check them out before I clicked on the appropriate name and proceeded to the next one. There were some photos I hadn't seen before, and they made me smile: some were goofy, from a late-night party one of my friends had while I was traveling; some were adorable photos of my cousin's kids; and some were from the fun travels of my coworkers. I was struck by how pleasant the experience was. No other security feature on any other site had ever made me smile and, at the same time, given me a chance to catch up with my friends. I don't want to downplay the seriousness of online privacy and security issues; I understand their complexities. But Zuckerberg is always several steps ahead. Just as he knew that he had to expand his service beyond schools, just as he knew the introduction of the News Feed would change the way we connect with each other, just as he knew that launching Facebook as a platform was the right thing to do while others argued that the world wasn't ready, Zuck knows that the times of radical online transparency are coming, and he wants to make sure we are ready (and maybe help us accept it).

Zuckerberg is biased in favor of sharing. It is at the core of Facebook: "The thing that I really care about is making the world more open and connected. What it stands for is something I have believed in for a really long time. Open means having access to more information, right? More transparency, being able to share things and have a voice in the world. And connected is helping people stay in touch and maintain empathy for each other, and bandwidth."[12] Those beliefs are shared by many inside Facebook. The place is abuzz with a sense of higher purpose, the change in the world, and excitement to be a part of that change. One employee notes: "It shocks me that people still think [Facebook] is like a trivial thing. Like it's a distraction, or it's a procrastination tool. I don't get it. This is fundamentally human, to reach out and connect with people around us."[13] Another employee chimes in: "You get at most one—if you're incredibly lucky, two—shots, maybe, in your lifetime, to actually truly affect the course of a major piece of evolution. Which is what I see this as."[14] And yet another: "But Mark's vision is not that it's all happening in this blue-and-white zone that we built, but that it's happening everywhere. Literally everything you use could be a conduit between you and people around you. The television could. The GPS on your car could. Your phone could. iTunes could."[15]

Zuckerberg is so dedicated to his vision, he is willing to support potential competitors who pursue the same vision. In 2010, four NYU college students challenged Facebook's dominance by building an open-source personal web server that implements a distributed social networking service called Diaspora. Instead of ignoring or challenging them, Mark donated to the project, calling it a cool idea. "I think it is cool people are trying to do it. I see a little of myself in them. It's just their approach that the world could be better and saying, 'We should try to do it,'" he said.[16] This action is a perfect example of his consistency in sticking to his mission and showing true character along the way.

In 2010, Paul Butler, then an intern on Facebook's data infrastructure engineering team, decided to initiate an interesting experiment. He wanted to track the locality of friendships on the social network. He was interested in seeing how geographical and political borders affected how people connected with each other. Taking about 10 million pairs of friends from Facebook's data warehouse, he merged different data points, like the longitude and latitude of each city, and ultimately drew the lines between them weighted by the number of connections. What emerged was amazing—a map of the world. And not a map like any other, but a map of human relationships in which each line represents a meaningful human connection with its own unique story. It was true reaffirmation of the impact Facebook has in connecting people across the world.

> **Successful leaders are purpose driven but they also have the courage to stand by their vision and execute on their convictions, no matter the external pressure.**

In October 2012, to celebrate reaching an extraordinary milestone—1 billion people on Facebook—the company revealed its first ever TV spot, "The Things That Connect Us." The message of that video:

> Chairs. Chairs are made so that people can sit down and take a break. Anyone can sit on a chair. And if the chair is large enough, they can sit down together. And tell jokes. Or make up stories. Or just listen. Chairs are for people. And that is why chairs are like Facebook.

Doorbells. Airplanes. Bridges. These are things people use to get together so they can open up and connect about ideas, and music, and other things that people share. Dance floors. Basketball. A great nation. A great nation is something people build so they can have a place where they belong. The universe. It is vast and dark and makes us wonder if we are alone. So maybe the reason we make all of these things is to remind ourselves that we are not.

The ad spot got people talking. Some loved it; some didn't. Some felt a deep emotional connection with company's purpose; some dissected every word. But what struck me is what Mark Zuckerberg had to say about the video:

Celebrating a billion people is very special to me. It's a moment to honor the people we serve. For the first time in our history, we've made a brand video to express what our place is on this earth. We believe that the need to open up and connect is what makes us human. It's what brings us together. It's what brings meaning to our lives. Facebook isn't the first thing people have made to help us connect. We belong to a rich tradition of people making things that bring us together. Today, we honor this tradition. We honor the humanity of the people we serve. We honor the everyday things people have always made to bring us together: chairs, doorbells, airplanes, bridges, games. These are all things that connect us. And now Facebook is a part of this tradition of things that connect us too. I hope you enjoy this video as much as we do. Thanks for helping connect a billion people.[17]

You can criticize the message in the video and dissect every little word, but the fact remains: Zuck and people at Facebook share the same passion, the same goal, the same vision. And they stay true to it as they work toward making a world a better place.

We shouldn't underestimate the power of passion and purpose. Mark Zuckerberg may be young, he might have made a lot of mistakes (and he is likely to make more), but here is a young person who is extremely sure of his vision and the change he wants to see in the world, and he has an entire company behind him that not only shares in this vision but acts on it every single day. That alone is an invaluable ingredient in the long-term success of a business.

Let's look at a few other businesses that lead with purpose—CollegeHumor, TOMS, and Threadless—and consider what their leaders have to say about the importance of having a clear vision.

If you like to laugh, you've probably heard about CollegeHumor.com. CollegeHumor Media is a leading online entertainment company targeting a core audience of people ages 18 to 49. Founded in 1999 by two high school friends, Ricky Van Veen and Josh Abramson, CollegeHumor Media delivers daily comedic content (videos, pictures, articles, jokes) created and/or curated by the CollegeHumor staff. The company's content attracts more than 15 million monthly unique visitors and, according to Nielsen, generates more than 100 million video views per month. A number of their original videos have been nominated for and/or won Webby Awards. The way the company makes money is through providing online advertisers across a variety of categories with an efficient vehicle for reaching multiple desirable demographics on their site.

Van Veen was 18 when he started CollegeHumor with his friend Abramson. He wanted to build something cool, something that would make him and others happy. In December 1999, Van Veen and Abramson were at a holiday party. Back then they used to DJ. They were not very good at it, but they did get paid. It was the height of the dot-com boom, and the boys were drawn to the start-up culture and—let's be honest—to the constant parties of the young founders of successful dot-com ventures of the time.

Those kids got to build amazing businesses and services, and it got the two boys thinking about the same. "So we did what we knew," Van Veen says:

> We were at the college at the time, we were freshmen. We created a website and started posting our funny videos and photos. We got some of our friends to write for us. Not only that, we aggregated funny content shared by others. We became one of the first user-generated content sites that aggregate funny content. There really wasn't much out there at the time. Josh and I both thought the same way, we are dedicated to it, and we wanted to see this grow.

The boys didn't have outside funding; it was just them working hard. They quickly realized that it was more satisfying to stay in and build something than it was to go out to a party or play a video game. They wanted to see how far they could take the site.

Then came a dot-com crash. The site survived because it didn't have any overhead or office space; Van Veen and Abramson were living in dorm rooms. By the time they graduated, the site had grown some, and the boys got to the point where they could do this for a living. "We weren't going to be rich, we weren't going to live too comfortably, but we would have pizza and cable TV," says Van Veen. "We decided to go for it." The two of them moved to San Diego. Two other friends joined them. Van Veen remembers:

> San Diego wasn't a very tech city. The measure of success for many people there was how little you had on your plate, while ours was how much you had on your plate. We didn't fit in. Because we didn't fit in there, we worked all the time. That was so crucial. We lived together, we ate three meals together, and when we weren't eating, we worked, and when we weren't eating or working, we talked about work. It was extremely effective. We came up with a lot of ideas. We got a ton done.

At that time, CollegeHumor exploded, and they started several other successful sites, like vimeo.com and BustedTees. The small team basically became a platform for launching new sites and new products. Some were successes; some were failures. The team of four became an idea and business factory because they had all the right skill sets in one place and a strong desire to see something come to life. In 2006, CollegeHumor Media was bought by InterActiveCorp (IAC). Ricky Van Veen, however, remains the company's CEO and continues to drive the business.

For Van Veen and Abramson, their goal was to create a humor site that would appeal to the college-aged demographic. Now that the company has grown, Van Veen says that at every all-hands meeting, the leadership team continues to reiterate the purpose of the company. Van Veen himself has a poster at his desk that displays the company's mission statement, "to create and distribute the world's funniest and most engaging content in innovative and trailblazing ways making our audiences and ourselves happier in the process." Everyone who comes into his office sees the poster. He considers it critical for the leadership to display the most important message front and center, because then that message travels throughout the company and is constantly executed upon. Van Veen also points out that you shouldn't be afraid to admit that the reason you are growing your business is to make money as well. He further explains:

> It doesn't mean you don't want to make money in the process. People in creative industries are almost allergic to placing "making money" in your mission statement, but happiness is only one of the reasons people work. They work for other reasons as well. You can make yourself happy because you are financially rewarded, or because you are being recognized for being innovative in your field, or because you are surrounded by like-minded people—that's all what "happy" means to me. And in terms of making the audience happy, that's producing great editorial content or getting people products they enjoy using.

After selling to IAC, the company was able to maintain its culture and its passion. According to Van Veen, it was a tricky thing to do, and they were very careful about it. When they grew to where they needed to move out of their cozy working environment into a larger place, the leadership decided not to move until they could get a whole floor to themselves to be able to recreate their unique working environment and their current setup. "We didn't want to give up our identity and our passion until we knew we wouldn't be at risk of losing it," said Van Veen. "Preserving our identity, our passion, and our purpose is what mattered the most to our continued success. You are nothing without it. If you just have a bunch of people coming to be there from 9 a.m. to 5 p.m. and not loving what they do or wanting to hang out with people they work with, your company is not going to go anywhere. It takes a cohesive group." One of the most amazing things about CollegeHumor is that it was able to maintain the feel of a small company. Everyone who works there considers coworkers their personal friends; they all still hang out together inside and outside of work. "We have great ideas coming at any hour of the day or night," said Van Veen. "We would be out at a bar or restaurant together, and people would write ideas on napkins in that clichéd way, but it happened because there was that singular group united by the same passion and the same goal who enjoyed being together. And this still goes on today." That is why Van Veen and his leadership team work extra hard to preserve their culture and align all business functions with their vision.

As Van Veen talks about the importance of knowing who you are and what the purpose of your business is, he also talks about ensuring that other elements of your business operate according to its purpose. Hiring people who are the right fit for your culture (which is shaped by your purpose) is one of the topics he brings up:

> It all starts with the passion and vision of the founders. From that, the purpose of the company gets defined. And once you have that, you need to ensure that every single member of your team is aligned with the company's goals. Most hiring in growing companies is done among a close circle of friends. You hire those you know because you

know you share similar values and vision, that they have the right skills, but they also fit within your culture. And if you know someone won't fit in, you have to cut it off right away. It will never work out. I have never seen it work out.

We will discuss the importance of hiring the right people and building the right culture in more detail in Chapter 3.

With its humorous, quirky, silly content, CollegeHumor has successfully managed to bottle the adventures of freshman year and serve it up to others in a fun way and, in the process, to make people happy. The company was able to transform itself from a goofy website to a successful movie-and-TV-production company. Considering all of the responsibilities of running a company, though, it is impressive to see that Van Veen not only recites the mission statement at every meeting, but he lives it every single day. He loves pranks and stunts, and he likes to make people laugh. An outgoing personality, he is always upbeat and smiles a lot. Whether it's hanging an "In-N-Out Burger Coming Summer" sign in Union Square for April Fool's Day or just lip-dubbing with his friends on camera, he always looks for ways to bring a smile to someone's face or at least to make people stop and ask, "Is this for real?"

When Blake Mycoskie told his friends, "I'm going to start a shoe company that makes a new kind of shoe. And for every pair I sell, I'm going to give a pair of new shoes to a child in need. There will be no percentages and no formulas," some thought he was out of his mind. Today, TOMS shoes can be found online and in stores of retailers like Nordstrom and on the feet of millions of kids in countries like Argentina and Ethiopia.

Blake Mycoskie is an entrepreneur who has started six successful businesses, including a door-to-door laundry service, an outdoor media company, a cable TV channel, and others. Teaming up with his sister, he competed on the second season of the CBS hit show *The Amazing Race*, missing the $1 million dollar prize by just four minutes. Mycoskie has a dynamic life, and he travels a lot. In 2006, while vacationing in South America, he discovered the alpargata, a traditional rope-soled shoe that has been worn by farmers in Argentina for centuries. Struck by the terrible poverty he saw there (kids developed cuts on their feet that led to disease), he decided to start a new company, one that would produce the shoes and not only sell them but give them away to kids in the developing countries. He found a manufacturer in Argentina he could partner with, then returned to the States and started his outreach. People immediately responded. They loved the idea and the cause.

Mycoskie decided to name his new company TOMS. He played around with the phrase "Shoes for a better tomorrow," which then became "Tomorrow's Shoes," and then TOMS. That name held a promise, a purpose. Blake says that his mission was his desire "to eliminate unnecessary human suffering through the distribution of new shoes."[18] He continues: "I believe each of us has a mission in life and that one cannot truly be living their most fulfilled life until they recognize this mission and dedicate their life to pursuing it. Sometimes a mission lasts for two weeks or two months, or possibly 20 years."

To date, TOMS has given millions of new shoes to children in over 40 countries. In 2011, TOMS announced its second one-for-one product, TOMS Eyewear, which helps to save and restore sight through prescription glasses, medical treatment, or sight-saving surgery.

When you hear Mycoskie talk, you hear themes of significance and simplicity running through his presentations. He talks about people's need to create or do something that matters, to build something of significance. And he talks about the necessity to just start, go do it. People use lack of money as an excuse, he says, but he started TOMS with $5,000 of his own investment. He also talks about keeping it simple. Instead of adding bells and whistles and complicating the heck out of the product, he suggests instead getting down to basics, asking yourself, "What is the one thing I am trying to say or do or sell?" so that people can understand it better. Once they understand it, they can share it or, better yet, join in. To have clarity of purpose is crucial to your success. It's even more essential to be able to articulate your purpose so that it is easy to grasp. The purpose of TOMS is to put a pair of shoes on every child in need, and the company has been working toward that goal relentlessly ever since its inception.

In the offices of TOMS, you can see the word *give* everywhere. Constructed out of different shoes, painted on posters, and translated into multiple languages, the word *give* is at the center of the firm's philosophy. As Blake Mycoskie told an audience at the South by Southwest conference in 2010, "When you incorporate giving into your business in a really authentic and transparent way, your customers become your greatest marketers. It's amazing!"[19] He has never forgotten how he experienced this for the first time. Four months after he started TOMS, Mycoskie was in New York's JFK airport, rushing to catch his flight. He got to the American Airlines check-in counter. He wasn't wearing TOMS that day, but as he looked down, he saw a girl in her midthirties standing next to him wearing a red pair of TOMS. Up until that point, he had never seen a stranger wearing TOMS shoes. He had to ask her about the shoes. "Excuse me, ma'am," he said. "What are those shoes?" She told him they were TOMS. When he didn't respond, the girl literally grabbed his shoulder and told him that TOMS was the most amazing company in the world and that when you bought one pair of shoes, they would give a pair to a child in need. She was so passionate about the company, he had to eventually admit to her who he was. But he was struck by the passion of his customers. They shared his vision, and they were willing to not only support it but to tell others about it. When the purpose of your business is aimed at serving others, your employees and your customers will be willing to stand next to you in the execution of that purpose.

Threadless is an online community of artists as well as an e-commerce site. Artists create designs that then are voted on by the community. The best designs are printed on clothing and other products and sold all over the world. Designers whose work is printed receive generous compensation from the company. As of early October 2012, more than $5,250,000 had been awarded to artists, over 460,000 designs had been submitted, and the community had grown to over 2.2 million international members.

In 2000, two students, Jake Nickell and Jacob DeHart, started the company with $1,000 of their own money. Jake was 20 years old at the time. He was coming out of high school and was going to art school in Chicago. He was working a full-time job. "Any spare moment I had, I was hanging out on the art forum called dreamless.org," says Nickell. "And I got to know the group of those artists who were misfits, rebels, they were designers from around the world." It was an invite-only forum of 300 people when Jake joined; when the forum shut down, there were about 3,000 people:

> Even though I was both going to school and working, what I was really passionate about was hanging out with these guys. It was my community. A lot of them were working professionally as designers at the ad agencies, and dreamless.org was their creative outlet to have some creative work for themselves, the opportunity to create something they really wanted to work on. We would come up with an art piece and post it to the site for people to react to, or work on a lot of collaborative pieces where each one of us contributed a piece for a bigger project.

But there was no recognition or extension of sharing that creative work with the world beyond that forum. Nickell decided to submit a T-shirt design to an event in London. There were several hundred entries, but Nickell's design won:

> And that's when it clicked for me. I started Threadless literally one hour after that by simply starting a thread on the forum that asked the community to post their artwork as a comment to my thread, and

I promised the community to make T-shirts and prints with their design that we can all have. Instead of our artwork disappearing into a digital wasteland, we can all have these things. I got couple of hundred entries right off the bat from artists from around the world, and I chose five designs to print just based on everybody's comments. There wasn't a voting system just yet back then. And then I built an e-commerce site to sell the designs. I figured out how to charge credit cards and how to print T-shirts. There were a lot of things I had to learn for myself to make this work.

Jake's purpose is to empower the community of artists to share their artwork with people around the world:

The reason I built Threadless was because I was passionate about making art with my friends, and the purpose of Threadless was to get the artwork my friends were making onto real products that we can all have. I also wanted to give an opportunity to the world to see the amazing designs my friends were creating. That same passion and that same purpose exist today. Passion and purpose are linked for me.

The Internet is making the world a lot smaller. When I started Threadless, I never thought I would be shipping to the entire world. Right now, 60 percent of our orders go overseas. Threadless created a platform that allows artists to access a worldwide audience who loves their art and relates to their art and enjoys displaying it in anything they do. There is no bigger joy for the artists than to know that their designs are being used in everyday lives by people around the world as a form of self-expression. Artists whose designs do well with the community not only get to see their work displayed by consumers everywhere, they are also now getting paid for their best designs.

There is a culture shift now away from mass-produced products toward customization. Example: in music, the top-selling album of all time is Michael Jackson's *Thriller*, which sold, I believe, 104 million copies. In 2010, however, you'd have to total the top 100 albums for that year together to reach 104 million album sales. Or it used to be there were three channels, then 10 channels, then cable gave us 100, and then satellite gave us 500, and then YouTube gave us millions. That shift moves us away from mainstream to unique. Threadless does take advantage of that trend. With Threadless, you can have a new product or design every day that you could almost make uniquely your own.

It's a truly amazing business model in which both artists and customers are rewarded: artists get their art appreciated, and customers get to choose art that is uniquely theirs and that allows them self-expression. When I asked Nickell about the company's culture and how it operates, he responded:

> Our mantra is "Make great together." And there is a lot we mean by that. First of all, making things is really important to us. If you go into our office, which is in Chicago, it is an old FedEx distribution center that takes up almost the full city block. We have about 100 employees, and we do all of our fulfillment from Chicago to the entire world. And when you first walk in, there is a 5,000 square foot open atrium space that's filled with artwork and random things we've collected over the years that are meaningful to our culture. We do a float in the pride parade every year, and all the floats sit in the atrium. We have a huge T-shirt installation where we made one huge T-shirt made out of 100 regular T-shirts. We made all those things ourselves. Even though we spend most of our day at computers, we get away from our computers to make things all the time. And then the "great" part of "make great" is to try to do the best work we possibly can every day. It is in line with our business model, where only the best stuff actually gets made; we don't just print everything. We are all about the quality and doing the best work. And the "together" part highlights a very collaborative environment; we are in it together.

It is the same with our website. There are no competitive feelings when an artist uploads a design; it's a very supportive community. It isn't this design versus that design; it is more of a "What do you think about this design?" Artists collaborate with each other, give each other feedback, help each other get printed, congratulate each other on the winning designs, etc.

The academic world is perplexed by Threadless's business model. This is basically a company that doesn't employ professional designers, has never advertised, and has no sales force or retail distribution. Because the community members choose the designs, almost every product sells out. The whole business is built on the idea that the community drives innovation. You don't hear about such companies often. To Nickell, all of the company's success was just common sense. To him, it was a natural vision: make both artists and consumers happy by creating a platform that provides a win-win situation for both parties. He continues to stay actively involved with his community to this day. When people want to talk to Jake, they get Jake right away.

Every single employee participates in the community, responding to questions, even submitting designs. When hiring, Nickell puts special focus on finding people who share his passion to "make great together" and who understand the company's purpose. He says:

> We try to grow our employees within. Twenty to forty percent of our employees started in our warehouse. And a lot of those people we found within our Threadless community. I don't value experience as much as I probably should; it's more about how passionate you are to do the work and work closely with our community, because I myself always felt like even if I am perfectly capable of doing something, I am not going to do a good job if it's not something I am excited to do. And if I don't know how to do something and I am really excited about the project or passionate about my work, I'll learn fast how to do

it. Going back to me starting this company, I didn't know 95 percent of the things I had to do to make it successful, but I figured it out as I went because I wanted badly to make it work. And sometimes people who know how to do something but don't care are not as efficient and don't contribute as much as people who care but lack the knowledge.

In 2012, Jake Nickell felt compelled to write a blog post to the community entitled "Why Does Threadless Exist?" He wanted to talk about his passion and the company's vision, and he wanted to thank the community for sharing the same values and beliefs:

I've been at Threadless now coming on 12 years. I'm super proud of this company, what we've built and the decisions we've been able to make. At our last company-wide town hall, I talked with our staff about why we are doing the work we are doing and wanted to also share that publicly. It's why I'm still here, motivated to do something I think is important to the world. So here it is!

First of all, there is the reason why I started the company in the first place. It actually started as a hobby and I had no idea the potential it had. But the reasons why I started it were important and are still important to me today. Coming out of high school, I was really frustrated with mainstream consumerism . . . everyone going to the mall and just buying clothes with corporate logos on their chests. I hated it. No individuality. Everyone listened to the same music and wore the same clothes. It's funny, Gap logo tees were probably one of the biggest perpetrators here! Meanwhile I was starting art school and learning a lot about the internet. I became involved with a small but talented & worldwide group of design misfits. I spent every possible waking minute hanging out online with them, making things out of code or photoshop or whatever and sharing them. Starting Threadless was a way for me to take that to the next level and make things with other people that we could all have.

To recap the WHY of this stage of the company—this is when we found our principle, found something in the world that we wanted to change. We were frustrated with the way things are created and wanted to make them differently and more collaboratively—and the internet empowered us to do so.

Then, things started to get traction. People really connected with this idea. Artists all around the world were regularly submitting designs and we were quickly finding people to actually buy them. This really blew my mind, I didn't think there were a lot of people in the world that shared this principle with me but apparently there were. Also, we were starting to get a lot of attention from academia and technology and business media. This really helped us to gain confidence around the idea . . . start to realize its potential. But most importantly, this is the stage of the company when artist opportunities became real. In the beginning artists weren't even paid for their work and it was a very small audience so recognition wasn't a motivator either. But now we were paying meaningful sums of money to artists and giving them meaningful exposure.

The WHY of this stage of the company is that we discovered that this was more than a hobby, in fact it was, according to Inc magazine, "The most innovative company in America." We discovered we had the power to make an impact on the world with this idea.

Today we think we can change the world with what we are doing. We believe that we can make celebrating the stories and work of the individuals who make things an integral part of consumer culture. We can be the drivers of that change. Our partnership with Gap is a prime example of us getting in there and changing the status-quo. We're working with them and other partners to completely change the way things are done. We can apply what we've been doing all these years to all sorts of new products, open it up to new distribution channels and audiences through partners, have a major impact on how content is created and consumed. Our community is itching for it. The talent and size of the community of creators we've attracted over the years combined with huge, meaningful opportunities we build for them will become an unstoppable force.

> So at this stage of the company, the WHY of it is about becoming bigger than ourselves. It doesn't just have to be us making t-shirts and selling them ourselves. We can share this with the world and with other products . . . We have an incredible community of super talented artists and designers and we need to spread what's happening here into the world in a huge way.
>
> **To distill the WHY down to a sentence, here it is.** "Threadless exists to give the creative minds of the world more opportunities to make and sell great art." This started with a discovery of something we wanted to change in the world, became something attainable as we got traction and something that is actually going to changing the world with all this work we are putting in today.
>
> Stoked to keep pushing and thanks for being a part of the madness!

The blog post received over 100 comments. Many artists thanked the founder. One comment read: "I wouldn't be doing what I am right now without Threadless. It's been a force of nature for artists and designers who have truly embraced its potential." Another read: "I just wanted to say thanks to your hard work and dedication. You created an outlet for me and many other artists to get their work out to the masses, practice their craft or just come to enjoy the best community I have ever been involved in on the interwebs."

Threadless continues to be true to its purpose. There were instances when Nickell had to decline tempting offers from brands that didn't align with his vision of the company and the expectations of his community. Nickell doesn't proclaim himself a business whiz; he is just a guy who has passion and a purpose in life. And that purpose is to make great things and to serve others.

Steve Jobs once said:

The problem with the Internet startup craze isn't that too many people are starting companies; it's that too many people aren't sticking with it. That's somewhat understandable, because there are many moments that are filled with despair and agony, when you have to fire people and cancel things and deal with very difficult situations. That's when you find out who you are and what your values are.

So when these people sell out, even though they get fabulously rich, they're gypping themselves out of one of the potentially most rewarding experiences of their unfolding lives. Without it, they may never know their values or how to keep their newfound wealth in perspective.[20]

A clear sense of mission helps keep a person, a group of people, or a whole company moving forward and "making great together."

What is your purpose?

CHAPTER 3

PEOPLE

*I've always focused on a couple of things. One is having
a clear direction for the company and what we build.
And the other is just trying to build the best team possible
toward that . . . I think as a company, if you can get those
two things right—having a clear direction on what
you are trying to do and bringing in great people who can
execute on the stuff—then you can do pretty well.*
—Mark Zuckerberg[1]

*One thing that gets blown out of proportion is
the emphasis on the individual. The success of Facebook
is really all about the team that we've built. In any
company, that's going to be true. One of the things that
we've focused on is keeping the company as small as
possible . . . How do you do that? You make sure that
every person you add to your company is really great.*
—Mark Zuckerberg, 2011 Brigham Young University speech

There is no more vital factor in the long-term success of any company than the quality of its human capital.

A lot has been said over the decades about the importance of a good team. Whether you are a growing business or an established one, if you don't have a team that shares your vision, your dream, and your goals, the business will not be able to reach its potential. No matter how you look at it, no matter which field you are in, no matter how brilliant your ideas are, success is a team sport. You can imagine the most amazing products or services in the world, but it requires people to make your dream a reality.

No new revelations here. Nonetheless, there is a very small number of businesses that can truly boast loyalty, passion, and full engagement among their employees. In 2011, a Gallup poll revealed that 71 percent of the American workforce is "not engaged" or "actively disengaged." The poll stated that workers who are "emotionally disconnected from their workplaces are less likely to be productive."[2] Which means only about one-third of the workforce is actually enthusiastic and fulfilling its potential. Over the past decade, multiple researchers have found a strong relationship between employee engagement and company performance. Happiness and productivity of employees are linked to better customer service, higher product quality, safety, positive word of mouth, and higher profits. Not to mention the savings—turnover can be costly, especially in highly specialized roles.

The chief concern of any leader should be his or her employees' and company's values. There are several crucial pieces to the happy, productive workplace puzzle: company culture, employee attitude (and fit), and smart leadership. In combination, they create a perfect balance: an environment for successful growth of the business and positive professional and personal development of employees. Let's look at the key principles of achieving that balance.

For any endeavor to be successful, you need a team of people who share your company's vision, its purpose. Everyone within your company should have the mantra "One team, one dream."

When a company is just starting, it is often a case of several people who work together because they have a shared desire to achieve a goal; they understand each other effortlessly and are willing to do everything in their power to achieve that goal, to conquer their own Everest. However, when a company starts growing, it gets harder and harder to find employees who share the same bigger purpose or who fit perfectly into the unique environment created by the founders. That is when it becomes necessary for a company's leadership to be clear in shaping and communicating the company's culture.

In July 2009, Jeff Bezos bought Zappos for $1.2 billion, to the harsh criticism of many investors. Criticism is nothing new to this visionary; Bezos is probably used to it by now. The critics said that the online shoe company was overpriced, it didn't have a good business model, and it wasn't a smart decision. But while others were looking at Zappos's profit-and-loss statement, Bezos was looking at the potential of the business, at its culture, at its spirit. Here was a company that was outselling Amazon on some of the same items Amazon was offering for less. Why?

Tony Hsieh, the founder and CEO of Zappos, attributes the company's success to three key factors: excellent customer experience, company culture, and investment in employees' personal and professional development. "[They] are the only competitive advantages that we will have in the long run," he says in his book, *Delivering Happiness.* "Everything else can and will eventually be copied."[3]

Zappos's culture is unparalleled. It has been discussed in many books and classrooms. It is *the* business culture. Words like "happiness" and "delight" are not just buzzwords at Zappos; they are a way of life. Hsieh founded Zappos in 1999. By 2009, at age 10, Zappos debuted on *Fortune* magazine's 100 Best Companies to Work For list at position 23. By 2010, Zappos moved to position 15 and, in 2011, to position 6.

The company places such great emphasis on culture because its people are both its team and family. Zappos doesn't prioritize employees over customers or vice versa. The company puts equal priority on both. Think about it. What an extraordinary feeling to know that every single person in the firm (including yourself) has a true impact on the larger vision and that you and your colleagues work in unison to achieve the same dream. And no matter what, your leadership supports and empowers you. Wouldn't you want to be part of such a company?

At the age of five, Zappos was growing well and becoming a successful business. That's when the company's leadership decided to make company culture a priority. "We thought that if we got the culture right, then building our brand to be about the very best customer service would happen naturally on its own," says Hsieh.[4] One night, as the team educated one of its new hires about the company's culture in a bar over drinks, someone suggested that they should be writing down everything they were saying about the company. Tony thought it was brilliant. Why not ask all of the employees to write a few paragraphs about what the Zappos culture means to them and make it into a book? Thus the Zappos Culture Book was born. In the true spirit of transparency (which Zappos prides itself on), none of the entries are edited, except for typos. The Book includes the good and the bad so people can get a sense of what Zappos culture is really like. Every year, a new edition of the book is produced, which includes the perspectives of employees, vendors, partners, and customers and is made available to anyone (you can order a free copy at http://www.zapposinsights.com/culture-book).

But the creation of the culture book wasn't enough. The company was growing very fast, and there was a need for clarity, internally and externally, regarding the definition of the company's culture. Zappos leadership wanted to ensure that before, during, and after the hiring and onboarding process, each employee was very clear on whether he or she was a true fit for the company. The leadership team decided to come up with the list of core values.

It took the company a while to clearly define its values. And it took teamwork. Like everything of significance that's done at Zappos, the values were defined collectively. The leadership team turned to employees for their input in putting together the list. The original list had 37 core values (you can find the full list in Tony's book, *Delivering Happiness*). It was a long list, so the team worked hard to identify the most basic values that truly represented who the team wanted to be. It took a full year—with ongoing feedback from employees—for the leadership team to produce the final list. Why so long? Because they wanted the whole company to truly embrace those values and commit to them long-term. They didn't want the list of values merely to be hanging on a poster somewhere in the office, mentioned only during orientation training. They wanted every single person to live and breathe the values every day. It would be a list of values that would be used to hire and fire people.

Zappos's purpose is to deliver *wow* in everything the company does. Its list of values supports that mission. The company's culture is grounded in the Zappos Family Core Values:

- Deliver *wow* through service

- Embrace and drive change

- Create fun and a little weirdness

- Be adventurous, creative, and open-minded

- Pursue growth and learning

- Build open and honest relationships with communication

- Build a positive team and family spirit

- Do more with less

- Be passionate and determined

- Be humble

Over time, the company's recruiting department developed interview questions for each of the values. The company's human resources (HR) department is seen as the protector of its culture. As a result, the team recruits only those people who are a perfect fit for Zappos culture and whose purpose aligns with that of the company—to be the best they can be and to deliver a wow experience to everyone they touch. Many talented people wish to work for Zappos, but only 1.5 percent of all applicants make it through the rigorous cultural screening.[5]

If you have never heard of Zappos or doubt its excellence, you need only call its customer service, and you'll be provided solid proof of who it is. Whether you are pulling a prank and want to order pizza instead of shoes (like one of Tony Hsieh's friends did, just to test the quality of the company's customer service), or you are looking for directions, or you talk in third person, the Zappos service department will adjust to your style, address your every need, and treat you with respect. In addition to that, you'll be delighted with the free shipping and occasional surprise gift in your shoe box.

It doesn't matter what developmental stage your business is in; it is never too late to clearly define your culture and your values. Build your organizational culture around your company's higher purpose. The careful choices you make during the hiring process—choices consistent with your cultural values—can make or break your business. Errors, if not fatal, will take away from your differentiation and uniqueness in the marketplace and from the opportunity to be the best you can be.

One of my favorite Tony Hsieh quotes is: "For individuals, character is destiny. For organizations, culture is destiny."[6]

> Your company's culture (or the lack thereof) directly contributes to the success of your business. As a leader, it is your job to help define your company's destiny.

One of the best visual representations of a company's culture is XPLANE's culture map. Talk about putting culture on a map! The firm has done just that, literally and figuratively.

XPLANE is a Portland, Oregon–based design and consulting firm. Started in 1994 by Dave Gray, a journalist and information designer, the company became a leader in creating visuals that explain business concepts and ideas. In 2004, Dave Gray, the CEO and founder, Scott Matthews, creative director, and Aric Wood, president, got together to re-envision the company for the next 10 years. After a decade of operating as a boutique info design firm, they were ready to scale up to become a global firm. The leadership team went offsite to Half Moon Bay, California, to redefine the company's vision and strategy. In a way, they found the work of shaping and explaining XPLANE's vision fairly simple. The company had a clear purpose and vision; it wasn't hard to define it. XPLANE intended to become the world's leading information design firm, leveraging information design to drive change. But as the team spoke about actually executing the vision, they kept running into XPLANE's culture as a potential obstacle. They recognized that the culture they had wasn't necessarily the culture they needed to grow and evolve; it was insular, comfortable, a bit static—not the type of organization that would take on a changing world and evolve in advance of it. The company had acquired another firm based in Spain and was poised for great growth. The more they talked, the more culture became the focus of the conversation, so the three leaders started dreaming about the culture they wanted. What would it look like? How would people behave? What would customers see if they looked at it from the outside? As they talked, Scott began to sketch, and without planning to actually do so, they codesigned the XPLANE culture map, possibly the single most important and impactful innovation in their business.

Just as the borders of a country are defined by a map, their dream culture took shape. It comprised a highly empowered group of people who were intellectually curious, great sharers and module builders, and mutually supportive in a transparent and highly aligned organization. Fittingly so, the culture map was very visual (visual conceptualizing being the firm's bread and butter). The leadership team wanted to make sure there was no room for misinterpretation. After all, a picture is worth a thousand words.

OUR CULTURE

Who we are, how we work, and our core values

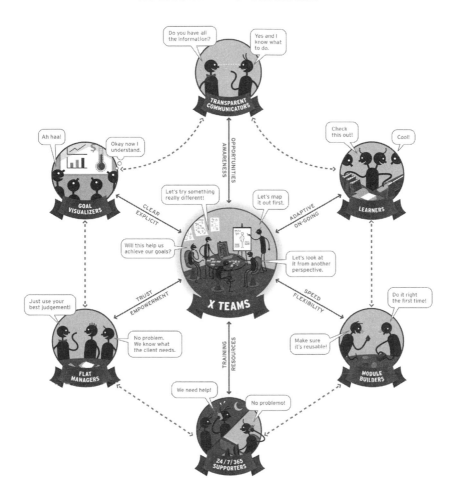

From then on, the XPLANE team used the map as a litmus test for every new hire and as a compass for all the critical decision-making.

"Our culture map clearly articulates who we are, where we want to go, and how we need to behave as we go there," says Aric Wood, current CEO of XPLANE. In our multiple conversations about business, strategy and long-term vision, Wood always lit up when we talked about culture and its importance to business success. He is proud of the fact that XPLANE's culture map hangs in every office, is shared with every new hire joining the company, and is frequently referenced in meetings and in conversations. Because the company grew very quickly, the leadership team paid special attention to recruiting new staff according to the culture map. Very soon, XPLANE's ideal culture became its true culture, and the entire team has made it their own.

XPLANE teams are key to the firm's success—they are in the center of the map. They are highly creative; they consistently push the envelope; and they help their customers think differently.

XPLANE's culture map has six key behaviors:

- **Transparent communicators**. Trust and full transparency are important to XPLANE leadership. They empower their teams to work independently and to make the right decisions. "You are the one on the ground," they say. "You know the customer and the situation the best." At the same time, leadership is transparent about key developments and opportunities that touch their employees. Company strategies, personal and team objectives, and even financial results are shared openly and frequently with the team, driving alignment across the organization.

- **Learners**. The agency values intellectually curious people, those intrigued by the new, the different, the unknown. Uncertainty is welcome at XPLANE; the traditional ways of doing things are challenged and, most of the time, turned upside down. It values insatiable curiosity more than experience, because change is a constant of XPLANE's work, and adaptability is a competitive advantage.

- **Module builders.** It is important to the teams to share their knowledge internally. They don't want others to reinvent the wheel. They want to share what works and what's "cool." Paradoxically, this doesn't create a static culture—it frees the team up to use the extra time to talk about new and different approaches constantly.

- **24/7/365 supporters.** "We are a team. And I am here to help!" That's the attitude valued at XPLANE. They all have the same mission and the same goal—to please their customers and help the company grow.

- **Flat managers.** There is a huge sense of empowerment. The teams in the field are closest to the issues and opportunities, and, if equipped with clear goals, no one is better situated to make good decisions, so decision-making is pushed down. A frequent mantra of XPLANE leadership to staff is, "I trust your judgment."

- **Goal visualizers.** Almost everything the agency does is visual. The leadership team sets clear objectives and ensures everyone has bought into them and understands them clearly. An example of this is XPLANE's strategy map. If you walk into any XPLANE office, you'll see the company's vision, its strategy, its culture, and often even its financial goals posted right out in the open for all to see.

Words like *adaptive, speed, flexibility, trust, empowerment, clear,* and *opportunities* can be seen on the culture map. Says Aric Wood:

> Our culture map is the most influential management tool in our business. It has had more lasting impact than anything else we've done. If a company's strategy is its brain, a company's culture is its heart—and strength, determination, values, and the will to win come from the heart. We grew 40 percent annually not because we had the best strategy, but because we recruited and retained the best people and developed a killer culture that perpetuated that cycle.

From 2004 until 2010, the company's compounded annual growth rate was around 40 percent. Even during the 2008–2009 recession, XPLANE was growing 18 percent, which the team is incredibly proud of. Says Wood:

I attribute our success to the culture we built (our people, our brand ideal) combined with mindfully balancing the needs of customers, employees, and investors—and never wavering from meeting the needs of each without over- or underserving any of them. Part of our strategy was to ensure that satisfied employees were as important as

OUR STRATEGY

Lead our industry by delivering WOW! to our customers, employees and investors.

satisfied customers and satisfied investors, and we actively measured how we were doing with each of those stakeholders so that we knew if we were meeting their needs or not. This rigor helped us to make balanced, long-term decisions and ultimately insulated us from the evils of short-term decision-making and "squeaky wheel gets the grease" business tactics.

What also makes XPLANE'S culture map visionary and relevant is the fact that it goes hand in hand with the company's strategy map. Here is how Aric Wood describes the strategy map:

> While the culture map describes who we are, the strategy map describes how we intend to achieve our vision. It, unlike the culture map, is meant to evolve over time. Above the ground, the tree represents what is seen from outside—a clear focus on balancing how we serve our three key stakeholders: customers, employees, and investors. For us, balancing the needs of all three is critical—if we overserve one and underserve another, the company (the tree) won't be stable and will eventually fall. So we solve for all—delighting customers, making the company a great place to work for employees, and delivering results to investors. This helps us make better long-term decisions, which requires making tradeoffs between the three. Below ground is what's not seen easily, and what evolves year by year: the specific tactics we employ to achieve our strategic goals for each stakeholder. We review this annually, based on progress as we move toward our vision, and revise as needed.
>
> Each company has a unique identity. It is critical to create a culture that supports the vision and purpose of the company. And it is equally important to ensure you hire employees who buy into your vision and display the qualities you are looking for. For XPLANE, those qualities are visually outlined on its culture map and are supported by the company's strategy, also visually represented on their

strategy map. Both maps perfectly fit together to paint a picture of who the XPLANE team is as a whole, what its values are, and where they are going. The maps provide transparency throughout the company and ensure that XPLANE's employees are fulfilling their potential. That, in turn, ensures happy customers, happy investors, and robust growth of the business.

Put your culture on the map, literally.

Though Facebook doesn't have a visual culture map, the "hacker" culture within the company is very well defined and understood by all. With almost 4,000 employees, Facebook continues to live and breathe its hacker culture, which allowed its employees to take the network from a simple student site to a worldwide enabler of personal and professional communication.

In his IPO letter (featured in Chapter 2), Mark Zuckerberg wrote: "I started off by writing the first version of Facebook myself because it was something I wanted to exist. Since then, most of the ideas and code that have gone into Facebook have come from the great people we've attracted to our team."

He then goes on to explain "the hacker way."

As part of building a strong company, we work hard at making Facebook the best place for great people to have a big impact on the world and learn from other great people. We have cultivated a unique culture and management approach that we call the Hacker Way.

The word "hacker" has an unfairly negative connotation from being portrayed in the media as people who break into computers. In reality, hacking just means building something quickly or testing the boundaries of what can be done. Like most things, it can be used for good or bad, but the vast majority of hackers I've met tend to be idealistic people who want to have a positive impact on the world.

The Hacker Way is an approach to building that involves continuous improvement and iteration. Hackers believe that something can always be better, and that nothing is ever complete. They just have to go fix it—often in the face of people who say it's impossible or are content with the status quo.

At Facebook, allegiance to the hacker way permeates every aspect of the business, from product innovation to organizational structure to management and training. For the first time, in the same letter, Mark Zuckerberg also clearly defined the company's five core values, which are consistent with the hacker way:

- **Focus on impact**. "If we want to have the biggest impact, the best way to do this is to make sure we always focus on solving the most important problems. It sounds simple, but we think most companies do this poorly and waste a lot of time. We expect everyone at Facebook to be good at finding the biggest problems to work on."

- **Move fast**. "Moving fast enables us to build more things and learn faster. However, as most companies grow, they slow down too much because they're more afraid of making mistakes than they are of losing opportunities by moving too slowly. We have a saying: 'Move fast and break things.' The idea is that if you never break anything, you're probably not moving fast enough."

- **Be bold**. "Building great things means taking risks. This can be scary and prevents most companies from doing the bold things they should. However, in a world that's changing so quickly, you're guaranteed to fail if you don't take any risks. We have another saying: 'The riskiest thing is to take no risks.' We encourage everyone to make bold decisions, even if that means being wrong some of the time."

- **Be open.** "We believe that a more open world is a better world because people with more information can make better decisions and have a greater impact. That goes for running our company as well. We work hard to make sure everyone at Facebook has access to as much information as possible about every part of the company so they can make the best decisions and have the greatest impact."

- **Build social value.** "Once again, Facebook exists to make the world more open and connected, and not just to build a company. We expect everyone at Facebook to focus every day on how to build real value for the world in everything they do."

Defining the values that will shape the culture of your organization is only the first step. Living that culture every day is no less important. And to do that, you have to find the right people who embody those values and execute on them daily.

In his book *Good to Great,* Jim Collins points out that good-to-great leaders "first got the right people on the bus, the wrong people off the bus, and the right people in the right seats—and then they figured out where to drive it." He writes: "The old adage 'People are your most important asset' turns out to be wrong. People are *not* your most important asset. The *right* people are." Two people can see the same thing but interpret it differently based on their life's purpose; they can be faced with the same opportunity and either take it or leave it based on their vision and their passion.

Finding the right people is easier said than done. Finding competent people is hard, but finding the *right* people is much harder. As Mark Zuckerberg puts it: "People can be really smart or have skills that are directly applicable, but if they don't really believe in [your purpose], then they are not going to really work hard."[7]

The *right* people are those people who share your beliefs, live your values, and strive for the same purpose. Those are the people who will see the changes coming when you miss them and help you look in the right direction. Those are the people who will stay with you when times are tough and give their best in the worst of times.

The first several years, Zappos struggled to survive; it was not cash-positive for a while. At one point, Zappos leadership decided to cut costs and lay off a small contingent of workers. Tony Hsieh remembers that those who decided to stay were true performers and true believers, and, as a result, productivity hasn't suffered at all. He recalls, "It was a big lesson in the power of instilling passion throughout the entire company and working as a unified team. Everyone was making sacrifices."[8]

To date, Hsieh thinks bad hiring has cost Zappos more than $100 million. "This cost is a result of not only the bad hires we've made, but the decisions those people have made and how they have contributed to additional poor selections."[9] Now Zappos has a well-crafted hiring process based on the company's values and focus. Discipline in hiring the right people is as important as company vision and strategy.

Zappos carefully builds in multiple questions and quizzes to test candidates. For example, one of the application questions asks: "How lucky do you consider yourself to be on a scale of 1 to 10?" They automatically filter out those who rate themselves below a 7, deeming them pessimists and, hence, not a good fit for the company's optimistic and upbeat culture. After all, they are out to find "happy" employees not only to create a truly enjoyable customer experience but also to represent the values of the company to outsiders (customers, vendors, partners, etc.).

Ricky Van Veen attributes the lion's share of CollegeHumor's success to a simple hiring practice: "I always hire people that are smarter than I am. If you look around at the people in the office, they do what they do a lot better than I could. It can initially be a blow to the ego, but it pays off in the long run."

Facebook's leadership team and Mark Zuckerberg himself understand the value of hiring the right people very well. From the early days, everyone at Facebook was involved in recruiting efforts. The company is on the lookout for talent every single day. Early on, the company set up a recruiting program and deeply involved all employees. Facebook's programmers did campus visits, tech meetups, and major tech events all over the country. Some (including Facebook's leadership team) used to stand outside of Stanford looking for engineers. Employees took the side job of recruiting very seriously. They even set up a wiki to share candidate names, and their feedback about them, as well as ideas on how to woo potential hires. Andrew "Boz" Bosworth, who taught Zuckerberg's artificial-intelligence class at Harvard and is now Facebook's director of engineering, says: "The people we hired were capable of solving the problems we knew were coming. You have to be prepared to jump in, make stuff, and grow."[10] It is enough to watch Facebook's recruiting video to understand the passion and true innovative environment that characterizes Facebook. Sometimes, the HR department posts coding puzzles on its recruiting page with the tempting invitation: "Solve programming challenges. Get a phone interview."[11] (You can watch one of Facebook's recruiting videos at http://www.youtube .com/watch?v=7Rp-JAFVwNs.)

The screening process at Facebook is rigorous. Joining Facebook's engineering ranks is especially tough. The applicant is first given a list of simple puzzles. If she makes the first cut, she is then given a list of more serious coding tasks. "There is no hand-waving your way through a coding interview," says engineering director Jocelyn Goldfein. "The most common reason for us to pass on a candidate is that they just are not up to the technical bar."[12] Those who pass the second test are invited to Facebook for a series of four tightly scripted interviews: two are purely programming exercises; the other two depend on the expertise of a candidate and involve "solving hard problems" and "engaging on a technical level."

There is one way to bypass this process—to become an acq-hire, someone who launches a company that gets noticed by Zuck himself or his leadership team. Over the years, Facebook has acquired about 30 companies, most of them with the purpose of getting the best talent, not the product. Zuckerberg says this approach is worth the price: "Someone who is exceptional in their role is not just a little better than someone who is pretty good. They are 100 times better."[13]

Facebook treats its employees well—free food, free dry cleaning, as well as a lot of other enticing benefits. But make no mistake—the key attraction is the company's culture and the vision of its leader. Zuck has "turned" many an engineer. For some critical hires, the conversation started with "No, thank you, I am not interested." But Zuck would then take the prospective employee on a long walk up a trail into the mountains (a tactic borrowed from Mark's idol, Steve Jobs), a walk that ended on a hilltop with a breathtaking view and the culmination of Zuck's pitch, perfectly timed. That walk completely changed minds and showcased Zuck's vision. The fact that Facebook's team is one of the strongest in the industry isn't the result of luck; it's the result of Zuck's strategic approach to hiring the best.

> **Develop smart hiring strategies consistent with your cultural values to bring the *right* people on board.**

The right people are not those who have the right competency; they are those who have the right attitude. Some of the most successful businesses have a nontraditional, strengths-based approach to hiring—hire the best talent first, then worry about finding the right role for them.

Facebook is one example of such a business. Facebook knows how valuable the right people are. A lot of times, they hire engineers for their skills and their vision of the future. Once a new hire is in the office, wondering what his responsibilities are, his instructions will be something along the lines of, "Take a look around, figure out what the problems or opportunities are, and help bridge them." The company encourages its workers to form teams around projects they're passionate about, because Facebook's leaders clearly understand that great work comes out of doing what you adore. Not only does this approach ensure that employees give their best to the project, but it also provides opportunities for career growth based on smarts and competence, not on credentials. In that sense, everyone is equal. You are recognized and respected based on your contributions to the improvement of the product; your résumé or your age doesn't matter. Facebook is a company where ideas turn into products whether you are an intern or the CEO himself. "Pixels talk," says Joey Flynn, one of the designers of Timeline. "You can do anything here if you can prove it."[14]

The flat management structure at Facebook supports that approach. There are very few vice presidents. Matt Cohler, Facebook's fifth employee, says: "We were determined to keep things as flat as possible. The harder we make it for people to invent together, the faster we fall behind."[15] Boz concurs: "God forbid we spend a single day not trying to prepare for tomorrow's Facebook. You've seen company after company that rose to greatness struggle with scale, struggle with culture."[16]

> Offer your employees a nontraditional career path
> that is based on their contributions and value-based behaviors
> and not on their age or credentials.

What's more, the best leaders recommend hiring outside of the industry. An outside look can offer a fresh perspective and often reenergizes the company. Steve Jobs was one such leader. He said: "Part of what made the Macintosh great was that the people working on it were musicians and poets and artists and zoologists and historians who also happened to be the best computer scientists in the world."[17]

Southwest Airlines is another company that believes in hiring outside of its industry in order to find the right people. The strategy must be working. For the past 40 years, Southwest has been challenging the conventional wisdom successfully. Despite being one of the smaller airlines,

Southwest has not only stayed in business, but prospered, becoming a customer favorite and an industry darling. Sherry Phelps, top executive in the People Department, explains the company's hiring philosophy: "The first thing we look for is the 'warrior spirit.' So much of our history was born out of battles—fighting for the right to be an airline, fighting off the big guys who wanted to squash us, now fighting off the low-cost airlines trying to emulate us. We are battle-born, battle-tried people. Anyone we add has to have some of that warrior spirit."[18]

Southwest's HR department prefers to recruit teachers, waiters, and police officers as opposed to airline industry veterans. "We would rather take an eager, hungry, customer-oriented mind and mold it to what works well at Southwest, than try to change the habits of someone who's come up through an organization that views life differently," Phelps says.[19] Every now and then, Southwest hires employees of other legacy airlines. But according to Phelps, it doesn't happen as often as anyone might think. Southwest is a brand that understands what makes its employees tick and what attributes it is looking for in a new hire. And that attribute isn't necessarily prior airline industry experience.

In 1962, John F. Kennedy visited the NASA space center. He noticed a janitor who was deep in his work, sweeping the room the president was touring. Kennedy greeted the man: "Hi. I am Jack Kennedy. What are you doing here?" Without any hesitation, the janitor responded: "I am helping put a man on the moon, Mr. President."

> Hire for attitude. Skills can be taught; passion can't.

One of the biggest advantages of hiring the best people is the fact that they don't need to be managed. They need to be empowered, but not managed. Oftentimes—and I've seen this a lot in my career—managers tend to spend most of their valuable time babysitting their weakest people and not enough time with their strongest. Even though the best people don't need to be managed, they do need a leader's time to discuss new ideas, present prototypes, ask for advice, and receive guidance on the direction they are moving in.

Note I said "guidance," not "mandate." Putting full trust in your employees and empowering them is one of the highest motivators there is. The role of a leader is not to come up with every single great idea for the company, but to create an environment in which amazing ideas can be born. Creating such an environment not only guarantees innovation in good times, it also continues to motivate when the company faces hard times.

Zappos fully embraces the idea of empowering employees. Its service department doesn't utilize a script. Each one of its employees is empowered to engage with customers online via social networks, and unlike the rest of the industry, Zappos celebrates the longest customer service calls, not the shortest. (The longest call on record was almost six hours long!) The company's CEO has almost blind trust in his employees. When asked by employees if he would participate in a video by dressing up as a nurse, he agreed without asking what the video's purpose was. That is how he ended up playing a nurse in Zappos's benefits video, which was presented to all of the company's employees.

Gary Vaynerchuk is a successful serial entrepreneur who has built his family's local liquor store into a national industry leader. In his book, *The Thank You Economy*, he points out the importance of focusing not only on your customers' happiness but on your employees' happiness as well: "I care more about my employees than I do about my customers, and I care more about my customers than I do about breathing."[20] That is what made him so successful. He continues: "The first thing that makes an employee happy is being treated like an adult. That means that until people prove that they can't be trusted, they should be allowed to manage their job as they can see fit."[21] That idea of trust is built not only into his management style but into the benefits the company offers—more precisely, the vacation time policy. Or rather, the lack of it. Vaynerchuk believes that employees will take as much time off as needed or required by their lifestyle and their life situation in any particular year. There are some who take more time off, and there are some who barely take any time off. But the result is the same: full dedication of employees, continuous joy in the workplace, and workers who give 110 percent to their employer. Simply amazing! Have you ever heard of unlimited vacation time? If you had access to such a benefit, how would you use it?

My past manager, Jane Price, who is retired from Intel and is now an executive coach, taught me an important leadership lesson: "Give people step-by-step instructions and you can expect to be satisfied with the results of their work. But give them a high-level problem with some guidance on what success might look like and empower them to dream up their own solution to it, and you will most likely be wowed by their imagination and appreciate the additional benefits to business that come with it."

A true leader doesn't breed managers, she breeds leaders. Johan Jervoe, vice president of marketing at Intel, told me once: "My goal as a leader is to work myself out of a job." His goal as a leader was to create a strong, self-sustained team that could be empowered to make decisions and lead when he wasn't there. That is a true mark of great leader!

Open communication within a company is the product of a trust-based culture. Since the inception of Zappos, Tony Hsieh and his leadership team were very transparent with employees, sometimes to the extreme. Aside from news about the Amazon deal (which the team was required to keep private by law), everything the leadership thinks and does is an open book. Zappos executives offer frequent communication, share company sales reports daily, hold "ask anything" forums, and have an open-door policy. In addition to that, Tony often shares his thoughts and news about the company with the rest of the world on the Zappos blog.

It is also a two-way street at Zappos; there is always communication back to the leaders. It is a company where employees' feedback is highly valued. That is because Tony Hsieh knows that every interaction with anybody anywhere is an opportunity to get additional perspective and learn. Every month, the executive team sends out a "Five Second Happiness Survey." The survey asks employees to rate the following statements on a scale of 1 to 3, where 1 = definitely, 2 = sometimes, and 3 = not at all.[22]

- I believe that the company genuinely has a higher purpose beyond just profits.

- My role in the Zappos Family has real purpose—it is more than just a job.

- I feel that I am in control of my career path and that I am progressing in my personal and professional development within the Zappos Family.

- I consider my coworkers to be like my family and friends.

- I am very happy in my job.

Everyone has an option to complete the survey anonymously. But if someone chooses to add a comment and his or her name, Zappos leadership personally responds. Employees are also advised of any changes to be made as a result of the survey.

Feedback is a gift. Constructive input opens new possibilities not seen by others (and sometimes not even by the leader). It fosters a discussion and can inspire creative brainstorms. No one has all of the answers or sees all of the opportunities. Executives must create a safe environment for heated discussions. In turn, that breeds trust.

Times of struggle have a way of keenly identifying the strengths and weaknesses of an organization. And when an organization is under stress and has the ability to rise above it, the root cause of its success becomes apparent. Aric Wood of XPLANE remembers that when clients stopped paying their bills during the recession in 2008 and the agency suddenly found itself in a cash crisis for a period of time, instead of jumping to cost-cutting from the top, the leadership took the issue to employees (transparency), shared data on the gap between goals and needs and actual income (clarity), and asked them to participate in the decision-making (empowerment) on possible solutions. Ultimately, instead of a larger layoff, the firm was able to save many jobs through agreed-upon across-the-board pay cuts and the deferral of some payroll. Once the economy picked up again, the company was much better prepared to recover quickly as it retained its key resources and capabilities. Another benefit: the shared trial of the times built trust and bonded the team even more closely. "Our culture map in particular led us to handle the situation much differently than other organizations, and we retained our workforce and continued to grow because of it," says Wood.

Mark Zuckerberg also aspires to full transparency in his leadership style. Every Friday afternoon, he holds open forums with employees and allows for candid Q&A. Not only that, Zuck asks others to share their own stories, ideas, impressions. He also keeps his word. Integrity is very important to him. One of the Facebook veterans concurs: "Mark has never missed a commitment he's made about resources he would give us."[23]

Employees' skills and competence are not enough. Only when they have full trust in a company's culture and its leadership will they take risks and give 110 percent to advance the success of the organization.

> Transparency and empowerment breed dedication, loyalty, and trust. Trust is the muse of unleashed imagination and unlimited innovation.

True empowerment also means allowing risk-taking and being okay with the occasional failure. Personally, I am among those who believe that it's better to feel regret about something that has been done than about something that hasn't been done. But for that attitude to prosper within an organization, people inside it need to feel protected; they need to know that even if they occasionally don't succeed, their leadership will have their back. In turn, they will respond in kind.

The whole Facebook culture embodies this principle. That is because Zuck believes in continued improvement in the quest for absolute excellence. He is not about to repeat mistakes of others, like allowing fear to encumber innovation: "A lot of companies are set up so that people judge each other on failure. . . . So many businesses just get so worried about looking like they might make a mistake that they get afraid to take any risks."[24]

The engineer-to-user ratio at Facebook is impressive. Zuck says that each engineer is responsible for at least a million users, and this is a point of pride for him. He strives to make Facebook the most intuitive, easy-to-use site in the world, with every single feature to support his purpose—to make it natural for people to connect with each other. That is why it is especially important to empower each one of his employees to make the right decisions without fear of repercussions. Each idea counts. Every piece of feedback is heard. Every person is positioned to make an impact. Every engineer (whether an old-timer or a newbie) is empowered to push her code live. Even though Facebook supports weekly updates, if an engineer really wants to test his idea, he can push a code update live to a group of users to gauge their reaction.

Facebook is an entrepreneurial environment, and every person within the company is treated like an entrepreneur and a creative thinker. If one wants to stay agile and responsive to the changes in the marketplace, that's the only way to go. It is definitely true for Zuck—staying nimble and innovative is critical to him. And the culture he created—a culture of doing things fast, taking risks, and not being afraid to break things to make them better—is proof of that.

> **Breed a culture of fearlessness, not fear.**
> **Fear destroys cultures and cripples leadership.**

Having clear purpose, a strong list of values, and a culture map is a great start. But without truly institutionalizing a culture map, it will become nothing more than a poster everyone starts ignoring after a while. Institutionalizing your culture takes time. It requires weaving your core values into the fabric of your enterprise, into your decision-making, and into your key processes.

Facebook does so marvelously. This code-led organization holds boot camps and hackathons, shifts people around to work on projects based on their interests, and sometimes mandates all-nighters.

Andrew Bosworth is Facebook's old-timer. He helped build some of Facebook's star features, like the News Feed. He is also the guardian of the hacker way. He was the one who created Bootcamp, a six-week initiation program for new engineering hires to teach them how to "think like Zuck," to teach them the Facebook way. After a short orientation, newbies are given a computer and a chair. They get an e-mail that welcomes them to the company. They also get small tasks of fixing bugs on the Facebook site. And yes, once the fix is determined to work, they are empowered to push the change live—an idea that is rather terrifying for a lot of them. But that is daily life at Facebook, and independence, initiative, and creativity are expected from each one of company's employees. There isn't just one way to solve a problem, and everyone is expected to speak up about his or her own approach to solving it. "It's free form [here]," says Boz. "If you're not coming up with new ideas, then you're just along for the ride."[25] Encouraging new ideas is critical to Facebook leadership, and the best new ideas are presented to Zuck himself.

Every 18 months or so, engineers are required to rotate and work on something different for a while. This requirement constantly brings new perspectives and experience to the teams and ignites new ideas. Zuckerberg himself prefers to be tightly involved in the creation process. He walks around to see what different groups are working on and holds office hours. He has a strict open-door policy—anyone can pop in and run an idea or a mock-up by him at any time he is around. And healthy dissent is encouraged—if you can defend your point of view (preferably with a mock-up). At Facebook, code wins arguments. The company values those who don't give up even if they are told no. Boz say that Zuck is only "happy to be proven wrong."[26]

Facebook also holds hackathons, monthly all-nighters where any idea or project can be brought forth for others to work on. It is considered an intellectual and creative exercise. Even company lawyers come to hackathons to watch the ideas fly and the creative process unfold. The company provides food and beer; engineers, their ingenuity. These events are usually not prescheduled. Most of the time, someone says, "Hey, are you guys up for a hackathon?" Word spreads. Others get on board and set the date. The only rule is that during hackathons, one can work only on someone else's project. Some of the most popular site features, like chat, video messaging, and Timeline, came out of these all-nighters. You get a feature to prototype, get it evaluated by Zuck and others, and, if approved, you get it launched. Hackathons also provide visibility for the projects and hard work of others. "It's easy to think you are the only one doing something important if you don't know how tough everyone else's projects are," says Bosworth.[27] Pedram Keyani, engineering manager of Facebook's site integrity team, puts it like this: "Imagine if you didn't have to worry about scale; what product can you build? Imagine not being constrained by processing speed; what can you develop? For us, hacking is about passionately working toward a goal and not being afraid of failure."[28]

Heated conversations that look more like sparring are not unusual on campus. "And we definitely fight. We expect people to be passionate, and they're going to fight to make their case," says Boz.[29] One can often hear the words "fight," "impact," "hack," "entrepreneurial," "keep shipping," and even "domination" on the Facebook campus. That is the spirit that is expected at Facebook. Nothing and no one ever sits still in the continuous pursuit of challenging the status quo. Facebook's values of "focusing on impact," "moving fast," and "being bold and open" really come to life and contribute to "building social value."

Justin Rosenstein, who left Google for Facebook, once described Facebook as the "company where large numbers of stunningly brilliant people congregate and feed off each other's genius. [The] company that's doing with 60 engineers what teams of 600 can't pull off." Then he goes on to say, "Everyone [at Facebook] is a total rock star, and everyone is happy and excited and passionate. We're able to launch a massive amount of cool stuff very quickly. I like that I can have a personal relationship with the founders of the company. I can walk over and talk to them about my thoughts and concerns at two in the morning. There's a neat synthesis of top-down strategy and bottom-up product development at Facebook."[30]

Facebook's dedication to staying nimble is also seen in its corporate offices. They are not finished. "The office looks unfinished on purpose," said Charles Dowd, Facebook's developer support manager. "It's a reminder that everyone is on a journey, and we haven't ever arrived yet. It gives people so much energy and freedom to take risks."[31] Mark didn't want the offices to feel corporate, so he requested that the original graffiti murals done in the early Facebook days be cut from the walls of the old office and displayed on the walls of the new one. Personal expression is welcomed in decorating work spaces. But what you most notice are little reminders of the company's purpose everywhere: in the artwork, the posters, the conference rooms, the drawing boards, etc. "When you are in an environment where everyone has a common vision, it's easier to get things done," adds Dowd.[32]

Truly committing to your culture also means feeling comfortable sharing it with the outside world. Aric Wood says that before the company moved offices, XPLANE had a hall of pride. The hall was central to the design of the offices, and every time they offered an office tour for new employees, vendors, or customers, there was always a stop in that hall. On one wall hung the agency's culture map and strategy map; on the other, all of the awards the firm had won over the years by executing on its strategy and its values every day. The XPLANE team is now looking to recreate the same structure in their new offices. Likewise (as previously mentioned), Zappos is very open in sharing its Culture Book with anyone who is interested in getting a copy.

> Building a culture takes time.
> Institutionalizing it long-term takes even longer.
> Be patient, be deliberate, be fair, and lead by example.

We've talked about "getting the right people on the bus." But what about "getting the wrong people off the bus"? A company with a strong culture is as good at firing people as it is at hiring them. Facebook and Zappos are excellent examples.

Facebook (and Zuck personally) has made some hires that either weren't the right fit or were simply outgrown by the company. Sean Parker was the company's first president. During his time at the helm, he helped raise several rounds of outside capital as well as keep Zuck focused on the important things. Burned in the past himself, Parker was the one who convinced the founder to keep the company private and maintain control throughout the years. That turned out to be a valuable insight for Mark. But Parker wasn't always reliable. And his penchant for getting into trouble brought too much negative press to the company. At some point, the board (on which Mark held a majority of seats) decided to ask Parker to leave the company (though the two didn't end their friendship and still stay in touch).

Owen van Natta, a former Amazon executive, was hired to manage Facebook's business development and was later promoted to chief operation officer. He brought his tough negotiating skills to the table and helped set up the operations side of the business, building up the sales and finance teams and increasing revenues substantially (from $1 million to $150 million). He also created Facebook's first strategic plan. But after a while, he started to get restless. He pushed too hard for a sale to Yahoo and didn't show long-term commitment to Facebook's vision. He didn't last long after that. Doug Hirsch, the vice president of product, was also let go for the same reason after only four months at the company. He didn't understand

Facebook's mission and disagreed on some of the key upcoming critical feature introductions and changes.

At Zappos, after the initial training and your first three weeks on the job, if you decide that the company's culture is not for you, the firm gives you up to $4,000 walking money to leave. The amount varies with economic conditions but is nevertheless quite generous. Why would Zappos do that? The offer gives new hires an opportunity to decide if Zappos is the right environment for them and whether they'll be able to not only enjoy their job but to delight others while performing their duties. And it gives Zappos an opportunity to let go of those who will not be giving the company their best. Approximately 2 percent of new hires take the offer.

> **Being rigorous about firing the wrong people is as critical as being rigorous about hiring the right ones.**

For most of us, compensation isn't the strongest motivator or a primary aspiration. Most of all, we want to love what we do and grow personally and professionally. A study published in the summer of 2012 in the *Harvard Business Review* looked at the main reasons young top performers are leaving their places of employment. Researchers found that high achievers who are 30 years old on average with great educational and professional credentials are leaving their employers after an average of 28 months.[33] This isn't the first study to show that younger people have no intention of sticking around if they don't feel like they are continuously learning and growing in their job. The companies that don't provide training opportunities, career counseling, and mentorship see more turnover than those that do.

Zappos is a company that offers its employees the opportunity to excel both personally and professionally. The company offers only average salaries to its employees, but it makes up for that in creating an amazing work environment. Zappos invests the difference between what it pays and what some other employers pay into activities that build the company's culture and promote employees' happiness. Zappos offers employees one of the best health plans around. It has quiet rooms to take day naps in. It also provides employees with free meals—not to offer a nice perk, but because they want their managers and their staff to engage with one another over meals, to get to know each other better, to make friends. Community building and creating an energized and fun workplace is important to Zappos. One of the members of the Zappos Kan Du team describes its purpose: "We at Kan Du are willing to do anything, anytime, and whatever it takes to improve the quality of life for Zapponians. You can come and ask us for anything. We will look for ways to say yes and put systems in place to make it happen."[34]

Whitney Johnson, author of *Dare, Dream, Do: Remarkable Things Happen When You Dare to Dream*, believes that people's dreams matter. "Far too often, we think of our employees as a sentient version of [property, plant, and equipment], looking to drive productivity as if people were automatons," she says. "Yet the real returns are to be had when we remember that every employee . . . carries a secret dream hidden in their hearts, and we as employers invest in and harness the power of those dreams."[35] Zappos understands the power of personal dreams like no other business. The company puts a lot of emphasis on employees' personal development. In addition to custom training, a huge library, and various educational events, Zappos has "the coach," or an official dream manager. The coach provides personal one-on-one coaching to staff members targeted at helping to increase the "happiness" level of employees. Most of the time, the goals that employees have are of a personal nature. And that's okay with Zappos. Their mantra is, "Happy employees, happy customers." Whether the employee dreams of composing better music, becoming a better cook, or being a better salesperson, the coach helps the employee find the drive to achieve her goals. If your employees are developing and growing, so is your business.

Dale Carnegie once said, "People rarely succeed unless they have fun in what they are doing."[36] The way Zappos executives and employees blend fun into their jobs is a work of art. Remember Zappos value #3: "Create fun and a little weirdness." This value is one of the most adored in the company and one that is practiced daily. From the pinball machine in the lobby to the superhero wall murals; to the fun conference rooms by the names of Elvis, Betty White, and James Bond (each decorated appropriately, mind you); to Nerf gun wars; to "Bald & Blue" day, where employees volunteer to get their heads shaved by other employees; to seasonal festivals, everything is done to promote happiness and weirdness.

And weirdness encourages innovation; it forces people to think outside the box. When we converse casually and when we play together, we come up with creative ideas and experience togetherness.

According to two business professors, Christopher Robert and James Wilbanks, laughter is an essential element in the workplace. In their paper "The Wheel Model of Humor: Humor Events and Affect in Organizations," they suggest that funny incidents can have a cumulative positive effect in the workplace. Laughter is contagious, and it is a good "infection" to have within your business. Humor is one of the most intense positive emotions aside from triumph (which doesn't occur often) and sensual pleasure (which is typically not appropriate for a workplace). Humor, however, is extremely social and can occur rather frequently. The positive effects of humor include better health, increased cooperation and organizational citizenship, job satisfaction, and positive disruption (emotions that drown frustration or fear and instead allow for creativity and innovation).[37] All of these effects can impact a business's bottom line.

If you think organizational cultures that leave room for fun can't make money, think again. Chad Boehne, process manager at the Zappos Fulfillment Center, tells the story of how his team achieved a 20 percent increase in total unit count. His team set a performance goal. Chad, the manager, agreed that if the team reached that goal, he would dress up like a garden gnome and walk around the office parading his outfit to all departments. He isn't a tall guy, and he has a beard, so one of the teammates suggested this fun reward. Do you think the team achieved its goal? Darn right it did! "Rewarding people with a $20 gas card or in some monetary way honestly isn't as motivating to my team as reaching a goal and having me dress silly. So I'm all about unconventional team-driven incentives," says Chad.[38]

At Facebook, employees work hard, but they play even harder. Even though they keep long hours, they get together from time to time to play and blow off steam. On the Facebook campus, multiple conference rooms are equipped with musical and game equipment. Every now and then during the day, someone pops in to see if a room is empty and takes a break playing a game. And every now and then, Facebook employees get together for a day or a night of fun to laugh together, to share stories, and to hang out with their leader.

> A company's success is serious business.
> But introducing a little fun in the workplace makes for
> a happy and highly motivated employee base.

And one more reason to be obsessive about the happiness of your employees: if you want to create an extraordinary company, you have to fill it with extraordinary people. After all, people don't engage with companies, they engage with people. Tony Hsieh says: "A company's culture and a company's brand are really just two sides of the same coin. The brand is just a lagging indicator of a company's culture."[39] Your people *are* your brand. Customers can sense your employees' emotional state, level of motivation, and loyalty (or the lack of it). If you can build passion internally, you don't have to spend money on marketing. Your happy employees will delight your customers, and your delighted customers will tell their friends. Your employees are your first frontier for customer loyalty and continued word of mouth. People want to buy into a business that is making a positive difference in the world.

Scientists at Rensselaer Polytechnic Institute have found that when just 10 percent of the population holds an unshakable belief, their belief will always be adopted by the majority of the society. This is also true for brands. Your passionate employee base is critical to your success. Combine that with your passionate customer base and you have a movement.

Hsieh says that Zappos didn't used to have a marketing budget. They spent all their efforts on creating excellent customer service. When word started to spread, Hsieh started spending his time speaking, which he says also contributed to the brand's exposure. But mainly his marketing was done by his employees, who raved to their family and friends about the joys of working at Zappos, and by their customers, who raved about free shipping and out-of-this-world customer service. Seventy-five percent of Zappos's daily orders are placed by returning customers. Employee evangelism and word of mouth is a powerful force that is capable of creating loyalty and building movements. Your culture and your values shape the world's perception of your brand and contribute to sparking and maintaining that movement.

There are people walking around with corporate logos tattooed on their bodies even though they don't work there: Harley-Davidson, Nike, Apple, Coca-Cola, and others. Why do people do that? It is because they understand and relate to the purpose of those companies; they feel a deep personal sense of belonging; they are part of that movement. Damien Bayless is a service tech from Canada in his early twenties. He loves Intel and shares Intel's purpose of connecting people through technology and enriching their lives. On his first visit to Las Vegas, he went to a tattoo parlor and got a big blue Intel logo tattooed on his back. When people suspected Photoshop shenanigans, he showed them a video of the process (and yes, he was sober). Does he have buyer's remorse? "Absolutely not," says Damien. "I am a real Intel fan boy."[40]

Herb Kelleher, the visionary behind Southwest Airlines, puts it this way: "Employees come first, and if employees are treated right, they treat the outside world right, the outside world uses the company's product again, and that makes the shareholders happy. That really is the way that it works, and it's not a conundrum at all."[41]

> Your people *are* your brand. Each one of your employees is your brand's face, your brand's best ambassador, your best marketer.

I cannot not come back to Apple and its famous "Think Different" campaign. Not long after Steve Jobs returned to Apple, the iconic "The Crazy Ones" commercial aired as part of the larger "Think Different" campaign. What was less known at the time was that Steve Jobs wrote the commercial himself; he wanted to reinvigorate the company and inspire not only its customers but its employees as well. The version of "The Crazy Ones" that Jobs himself narrates didn't air until after his death. But by then, everyone knew it by heart. Here is what it said:

Here's to the crazy ones. The misfits. The rebels. The troublemakers. The round pegs in the square holes. The ones who see things differently. They're not fond of rules. And they have no respect for the status quo. You can quote them, disagree with them, glorify or vilify them. About the only thing you can't do is ignore them. Because they change things. They push the human race forward. And while some may see them as the crazy ones, we see genius. Because the people who are crazy enough to think they can change the world, are the ones who do.[42]

The strongest brands are those that not only understand the value of their human capital, but those that look for true trendsetters, game-changers, rebels who introduce energy and life into their organizations and cause healthy disruptions. The best-performing companies are those that allow their employees to shake things up daily and challenge the status quo constantly. They are not looking for "yes" men and women; they empower courage of conviction, freedom of speech, and action. Facebook, Apple, and Zappos are such companies. They are also companies that deeply appreciate their people.

On the tenth anniversary of the Apple Store, the company created a poster that was circulated among its employees. The poster's text addresses the creation and journey of the Apple Store—the place where the company touches its customers—and it addresses the successes and mistakes the Apple Store made. The poster also celebrates Apple employees, who are the heart and soul of the company. This quotation from the poster truly shows Apple's culture of passion, purpose, and gratitude toward its people:

> . . . And at the very center of all we've accomplished, all we've learned over the past 10 years, are our people. People who understand how important art is to technology. People who match, and often exceed, the excitement of our customers on days we release new products. The more than 30,000 smart, dedicated employees who work so hard to create lasting relationship with the millions who walk through our doors. Whether the task at hand is fixing computers, teaching workshops, organizing inventory, designing iconic structures, inventing proprietary technology, negotiating deals, sweating the details of signage, or doing countless other things, we've learned to hire the best in every discipline. We now see that it's our job to train our people and then learn from them. And we recruit employees with such different backgrounds—teachers, musicians, artists, engineers—that there's a lot they can teach us. We've learned how to value a magnetic personality as much as proficiency. How to look for intelligence but give just as much weight to kindness. How to find people who want a career not a job. And we've found that when we hire the right people, we can lead rather than manage. We can give each person their own piece of the garden to transform.[43]

To sum it up: hire the right people, empower them to fail their way to amazing things, and lead by example. And always remember, the secret to successful hiring is to look for people who want to change the world!

I cannot wrap up this chapter without talking about leadership. In building a successful company and a solid culture, smart leadership is a vital ingredient. It is the fiber that ties all other threads of the organization together. It is the DNA that permeates a company's culture and either makes or breaks an organization. And I am not just talking about founders or executives; I am talking about leadership at any level of the organization. Just as it is important to find the right people, it is critical to attract and, most important, cultivate the true leaders within your company.

We look at leaders like Estee Lauder and Steve Jobs, at their charisma and everything they've accomplished, and we call such people "natural-born leaders." But any leader who has ever achieved greatness will tell you that leadership is not a quality you are born with; it is something you learn as you go through life. Just look up quotes on this topic from your idols. For instance, legendary NFL football coach Vince Lombardi said, "Contrary to the opinion of many, leaders are not born; they are made. And they are made by hard effort."[44] Leadership qualities can be learned.

Another thing to note before we go any further in this chapter: When we talk about effective leaders, we automatically think of people like Oprah, Mary Kay Ash, Jack Welsh, Steve Jobs, and other great minds and entrepreneurs of our time. However, one doesn't have to be a publicly recognized figure to be a leader. And a lot of times, true leaders aren't even managers. *I define a leader as someone who has the respect and admiration of his peers and who has the ability to influence a group of people toward the achievement of a particular goal.* To me, the most impressive type of leadership is matrixed leadership, where one has to influence a group of people who don't directly report to him or her. If you look around your own workplace closely, I have no doubt you will find true leaders who don't hold the rank of executive, those whom others would follow if they decided to leave the team or the company.

Most of my life, I studied leadership; it is a fascinating topic for me. I shadowed the best leaders I met, I studied leadership gurus, I spent countless hours discussing this topic with both experts and random people. I drew not only from my experience but from the experience of others as well. And the more I thought about the qualities of the most effective leaders out there, I narrowed them down to a list of 10. This combination of the qualities forms what I call The Hummingbird Effect of Leadership.

Why hummingbird? The hummingbird is the smallest bird in the world. Different species of hummingbirds can vary in length from two to eight inches, with the bee hummingbird being the smallest—only two inches in length. This tiny flyer weighs about as much as a U.S. penny (approximately 0.1 ounce). For such a small bird, it is an fascinating creature. Early Spanish explorers called hummingbirds "flying jewels."

Hummingbirds can fly forward, sideways, and upside down, as well as hover in midair. And it is the only bird that can fly backward. A hummingbird's legs are not made for walking on the ground, so it prefers to spend most of its time in flight. As its wings can beat up to 100 times per second, it burns a lot of energy, which is the reason hummingbirds are constantly on the lookout for sweet nectar to maintain their energy levels. When a source of food is not readily available or when the bird sleeps, it conserves its energy by going into a hibernation-like state of hovering in midair, which forces its heart to slow down from about 1,200 beats per minute to 50–180 beats. What's more, some species travel 500 to 2,000 miles during migration in a nonstop flight. The rufous hummingbird has the longest migration of any species with a distance of more than 3,000 miles from its nesting grounds of Alaska and Canada to its winter habitat in Mexico.

These tiny birds have a chameleon-like ability to either blend in or stand out as necessary. They are able to flash their bright colors or hide them thanks to a prism feather structure (the iridescent coloring coming from prism-like cells within the top layers of the feathers). Hummingbirds are also extremely courageous. They are known to attack larger birds like hawks and crows when they violate their territory or venture too close to the nesting female.

Christopher Clark, a biologist at the University of California at Berkeley, believes that hummingbirds are capable of pushing the limits of what is physically possible. These tiny birds, he says, can sustain speed accelerations that would cause a fighter jet pilot to pass out.[45] A hummingbird's brain makes up a little over 4 percent of its body weight, the largest percentage in the bird kingdom. They are extremely smart: they remember every flower they have been to and know how long it'll take the flower to refill with nectar. They can see farther than and hear better than humans. If their brains take up 4 percent of their body mass, their hearts takes up 30 percent. They are the only birds that can pollinate certain types of flowers, and, in doing so, they maintain the beauty of the unique flora on Earth.

Hummingbirds are widely admired in the mythology of various cultures, and deservedly so. Aztecs, for example, wore hummingbird talismans to represent energy, vigor, and skills at arms.

Just like a hummingbird, small and unobtrusive, a seemingly ordinary person who might not stand out from the crowd can be a true leader. As a matter of fact, most effective leaders do not have the look or swagger of a big shot. They tend to be humble and shy away from the spotlight, preferring their team gets the credit. They realize that no matter how great you may be, there is always someone who is better than you at something. And they not only look to hire people who are more capable than they are; they reward and empower them. Executives at Zappos offer a perfect example of effective but humble leadership. Tony Hsieh is a very humble individual who always gives more credit to others in his speeches than to himself. Never does any person on the leadership team shy away from taking a customer's service call, helping out in the warehouse, or making a run for it to ensure that a customer's item makes it onto the delivery truck on time. Zappos executives sit in an area called "Monkey Row," with lush foliage surrounding their desks and bananas hanging in some cubicles. The executive team is hence referred to as "monkeys," a term that promotes humility and accessibility. (Remember Zappos value #10: "Be humble.")

Here are 10 qualities that make up The Hummingbird Effect of Leadership:

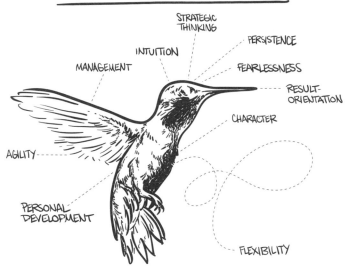

HUMMINGBIRD EFFECT OF LEADERSHIP

STRATEGIC THINKING

PERSISTENCE

INTUITION

FEARLESSNESS

MANAGEMENT

RESULT-ORIENTATION

CHARACTER

AGILITY

PERSONAL DEVELOPMENT

FLEXIBILITY

1. **Flexibility.** Just as a hummingbird can fly in any direction, a true leader has a good sense of adaptability. The hummingbird is second to none in its ability to maneuver in the air. Whether in leadership style, in strategic direction due to marketplace changes, or in the approach to problem-solving, leaders display flexibility while staying true to the core purpose of the company.

2. **Management.** The beauty of the hummingbird is in its flight, which ranges from hovering in the air to reaching high speeds. Even though speed is important, a leader also knows when to adjust, change the tactic or approach, or even slow down company growth, as we will see in the case of Mark Zuckerberg and Facebook in Chapter 4. Sometimes it is necessary to "hover" for a while before making the next acceleration. A good leader knows how to adjust the speed of "flight" appropriately.

3. **Agility.** The hummingbird is always in flight, restless in its constant quest for food. Likewise, leaders always look for continued innova-

tion; they never rest on their laurels and are on a constant quest for improvement, growth, and excellence. Effective leaders are wary of complacency and understand that sometimes the biggest obstacle is success—the bigger the company, the harder it is to stay nimble. Leaders cultivate the right environment for innovation and creativity to thrive in.

4. **Strategic thinking.** Similar to hummingbirds in planning their long trips and searching for food, successful leaders are highly strategic. In creating a long-term strategy that will stand the test of time, they are guided by their company's purpose and the best interests of its customers, employees, and investors (no matter how hard it is to balance all three). If well thought through and crafted right, a long-term strategy doesn't change for years. However, it should also be flexible enough to accommodate extreme changes in the marketplace and in the economy.

5. **Persistence.** Just as hummingbirds are capable of long, nonstop migration, effective leaders demonstrate persistence in their devotion to their company's purpose and long-term vision, sometimes seeing potential or end results that others might not. Such leaders don't waver from their course, oftentimes ignoring critics and naysayers. However, they are careful to communicate clearly internally and to share their vision consistently during the journey. They don't let failure define who they are; they prefer to fail over and over in order to achieve excellence rather than not to try at all.

6. **Fearlessness.** Great leaders are fearless in protecting their business and their teams. Just as hummingbirds have the courage to take on much bigger birds when the situation calls for it, effective leaders are constantly aware of internal and external threats, their strengths and weaknesses, and their competition. They are not obsessed with the competition; they stay in the know but spend most of their energy on reinvention and innovation rather than on figuring out how to

outsmart competitors. Great leaders are not afraid to make mistakes and always give their people full freedom to create.

7. **Result-orientation.** Just like the long flight of a hummingbird toward its migration destination, the road to an enterprise's long-term success is built on short-term goals and everyday results and accomplishments. Great leaders foster an impact-driven culture. But just as hummingbirds have a unique ability to preserve energy when necessary, effective leaders are careful to distribute their resources for optimal benefit on a long journey. In the process, they give people freedom to craft and execute tasks as they see fit, considering the right use of available resources (both human and financial) and, in the process, empowering them to succeed.

8. **Intuition.** A hummingbird can make a 3,000 mile journey relying only on its natural instincts and great navigation skills. Sometimes equipped with limited data and armed with only intuition and clarity of their company's vision, effective leaders can make decisions based on their gut.

9. **Character.** Great leaders always serve others first and foremost. Just like hummingbirds, effective leaders have a big heart. And a ton of integrity. They are authentic and credible. They keep commitments and are transparent in their intentions and communications. They demand accountability from themselves before others. They are trustworthy, and they extend trust.

10. **Personal development.** Effective leaders admit their shortcomings and always strive to better themselves professionally and personally. Similar to a hummingbird's ability to change the color of its feathers as life's situation calls for it, effective leaders are not afraid to learn and improve their personal style in order to grow. They are highly confident people and are not afraid to ask for help or partner with those who can complement them in various ways. They are

not above feedback; on the contrary, they develop feedback systems both internally and externally to ensure they are continually improving, and they act on that feedback.

The amazing qualities of the hummingbird can be seen in the beauty and complexity of its flight. Just like this flyer, effective leaders soar in their purpose of serving others and, in the process, achieve unprecedented heights of success.

In my opinion, Mark Zuckerberg deserves to be named among such leaders.

The CEO of Facebook is often described as "baby-faced." Interestingly enough, he sometimes remarks that he feels old. For the past eight years, people have argued that he is too young and inexperienced to run a company. That he is too stubborn in sticking to his purpose and not stubborn enough for his company to make a profit. That his introverted and awkward nature will never allow him to demonstrate the charisma that is expected from a true leader. But no matter what one thinks about young Zuckerberg, one cannot call eight solid years of his company's unprecedented growth pure luck.

Zuck is a minimalist. Even when he became a billionaire on paper, he continued to live a simple lifestyle. He rented small apartments with no fancy furbishing. He doesn't wear fancy clothes—his choice of attire is a pair of jeans and a hoodie. Ellen McGirt, a journalist for *Fast Company* who interviewed Zuck on multiple occasions, once called him "an odd mix of friendly, quirky post-teenager and philosopher king in training."[46] He would talk about his love of the Guitar Hero game even as he continued circling back to the topic of openness and connecting the world. He doesn't seem to get too passionate about money. What he is really passionate about is changing the world.

Zuck's style of quiet reflection, which sometimes can be seen as distant and ignoring, throws off a lot of people. And it doesn't endear him to them. He doesn't seem to care. Thanks to his depiction in *The Social Network*, people will forever see him as a socially flawed and greedy nerd. "He is shy and introverted, and he often does not seem very warm to people who don't know him, but he is warm," says Sheryl Sandberg, Zuck's right hand and Facebook's chief operating officer. "He really cares about the people who work here."[47] Mark's reaction to the movie that didn't seem to depict who he really is was rather even: "I don't think about it . . . much. I understand why people need to have these dialogues, to ask these questions. We have so much to do here, we don't think about it if we don't have to."[48] What makes people nervous, I think, is that Zuck is reluctant to reveal himself and offer any further details; he doesn't try to explain avoiding the spotlight and empty words. Some admire him for his confidence and his focus; some don't understand it.

By the accounts of many of his friends and coworkers, under Zuck's hoodie is a very assured leader. He is sharp, determined, and a hard worker. He is a sponge for learning—he asks more questions than he makes statements and continuously inquires, "Why?" And he has a clear sense of what he is good at (product design and strategy) and where he is lacking (day-to-day management and operations). To compensate for that, he hired sharp people like Ms. Sandberg and created a personal brain trust of advisors such as Microsoft founder Bill Gates, Apple CEO Steve Jobs, *Washington Post* CEO Donald Graham, Netscape cofounder Mark Andreesen, and others (some of whom also sit on Facebook's board of directors). Steve Jobs biographer Walter Isaacson says Jobs and Zuckerberg had a lot of mutual respect for each other. "I once asked Jobs who [he] admired in the Valley. Mark's was the first name on his lips. He felt an odd kinship to Mark," said Isaacson.[49] Jobs admired Mark's "intuitive feel" for where Facebook needed to go next and his passion and willingness to "do stuff that allows him to be on shifting sands—he is willing to cannibalize old things."

Facebook's leader is far from being the naive teenager he was when he launched Facebook in 2004. By now, he is tempered by both failures and successes. He doesn't wait around for approval; he moves fast and expects everyone else around him to do the same. He reportedly reached an acquisition deal with Instagram chief Kevin Systrom in a matter of hours in private over steaks and ice cream while lawyers sat on the couch watching TV. (Facebook bought the photo-sharing app for $1 billion in 2012.)

At heart, Zuck is a romantic. He is a fan of Taylor Swift, and he designed his wife's wedding ring (a small ruby flanked by diamonds on either side). He is also fearlessly dedicated to personal and professional growth. Every year, he sets a new personal challenge for himself. In 2009, it was to wear a tie for a year. On his Facebook wall, he wrote:

> My 2009 challenge was to wear a tie for a whole year. After the start of the recession in 2008, I wanted to signal to everyone at Facebook that this was a serious year for us. Great companies thrive by investing more heavily while everyone else is cutting back during a recession. But great companies also make sure they're financially strong and sustainable. My tie was a symbol of how serious and important a year this was, and I wore it every day to show this.

In 2010, the challenge was to learn Mandarin:

> In 2010, my personal challenge was to learn Mandarin. I have always been interested in Chinese culture, and learning a language is a great way to learn about a culture. Learning a language is also a good intellectual challenge, and Mandarin is a particularly difficult language for English speakers. I have had a hard time learning languages in the past, so this seemed like a particularly good challenge. Finally, some members of my girlfriend's family only speak Chinese, and I wanted to be able to talk to them.

Of course, there might be a little more to this particular challenge than Zuck lets on, given his plans for potential expansion in China.

In 2011, his challenge was to move toward vegetarianism and eat only meat that he killed himself: "The reason for this is that I feel lucky for having such a great life. I like eating meat, and before this year I ate it almost every day," he wrote. "In order to practice thankfulness, I want to be more connected to the food I eat and the animals that give their lives so I can eat them."

Says Marc Benioff, the chief executive of Salesforce, who has known Zuck for years: "What's most interesting about Mark is how he developed himself as a leader. Not only did he have an incredible vision for the industry, but he had an incredible vision for himself."[50] Once the company started growing, its founder realized that he needed to start acting more like a leader. He proclaimed he would stop writing software. On the weekends, he would read Peter Drucker. He asked his management idol, Don Graham, if he could shadow him. He spent hours chatting with Jobs and Gates.

Back in 2005, when Zuckerberg was approached with multiple buyout offers, the situation inside the company became tense. Rumors about selling ran rampant, Facebook's internal politics were getting heavy, and communications seemed to be breaking down. Mark didn't seem to notice and didn't bother to explain his thinking and his plans. A recruiter for the company, Robin Reed, remembers the dire situation they were in. One night she caught up with Zuck and asked to chat. She told him about her frustration and that the team was ready to mutiny. "You'd better take CEO lessons," she advised. "Or this isn't going to work out for you!"[51] Over the next several weeks, she noticed a real change in Mark. He agreed to start seeing an executive coach. He called for weekly "all-hands" meetings where he shared his thoughts and his vision with all of the employees. He started having more meetings with his executive team. The twenty-two-year-old founder showed admirable candor when he admitted to his team: "It may not make you comfortable to hear me saying this, but I'm sort of learning on the job here."[52] He readily owns up to his errors, saying publicly: "Almost any mistake you can make in running a company, I've probably made."[53] But he also works hard on correcting them and learning from them. His candor—with himself and with others—shows his character and is consistent with his belief in integrity and transparency.

When a business is small, it is easy to understand its purpose, borne out of the personality and vision of its founder. Because of the employees' proximity to the founder and the ease of close, clear communication among a relatively small group of people, it is easy to cultivate the spirit and culture of a small company. As an organization grows, it is vital to continue to communicate and inspire. The purpose and the original passion need to be integrated into the culture. And Zuck does just that. He is authentic. Authenticity is when you have a strong belief and you not only communicate it, you act on it. It's Zuck's authenticity and his personal vision that not only attract the best talent to Facebook but form the "cult of Zuck." Everyone I talk to at Facebook has the same belief and the same goal, they all fancy the same revolution, and they are all passionate about connecting the world.

In the next chapter, we will discuss the strategy behind the world's most popular social network, why Facebook is successful, and lessons learned along the way. You will see why the "cult of Zuck" exists, how he won over internal critics, and why he is an incredibly strategic leader.

CHAPTER 4

PRODUCT

*I believe that over time people get remembered
for what they build, and if you build something great,
people don't care about what someone says about you
in a movie . . . they care about what you build.*

—Mark Zuckerberg[1]

Facebook is fundamentally changing the way people communicate, the way marketers sell their products, the way people receive and filter news, the way governments interact with their citizens, and, in some countries, it critically influences even political regimes. The social network brings people together. It empowers them. It makes the world smaller. Its users span generations, languages, and geographies. What started as a college coding project by a 19-year-old became a technological powerhouse with enormous influence on people's everyday lives. Facebook may be the fastest-growing company ever. And that is because it is a company that places people, not technology or content, at the center of its business model.

Mark Zuckerberg has built an extraordinary product at the right time using the right resources in the most strategic way. Some call him lucky. Even though a little bit of luck is a necessary element of success, more than luck is required to imagine, build, and then launch a product that will appeal to your customers. If you have a clear vision, you are able to identify the path and the opportunities that align with your vision more easily and more clearly than anybody else. For centuries, people watched apples fall from trees and hit the ground, but only Sir Isaac Newton was able to define the law of gravity. If you don't have passion for something and a vision of where you want to go, you might miss the opportunities that come your way to make your dream a reality. Estée Lauder is credited with saying, "People do make their luck by daring to follow their instincts, taking risks, and embracing every possibility."[2]

It is my belief that three critical elements contributed to the successful launch and growth of Facebook: Zuck's passion, his clear vision of Facebook's purpose, and the people he hired (or partnered with) to execute on his vision. All three form a triangle of factors that, in turn, shaped the final product into what it became: a unique representation of Zuck's vision combined with the digital social needs of people around the world. A triangle is the strongest geometric shape and is considered by architects one of the ideal shapes in building their masterpieces. Just as an architect aspires to construct a building that will stand the test of time, an entrepreneur should build his product considering the three sides of the triangle. We've discussed three critical elements in previous chapters: passion, purpose, and people. This chapter brings those elements together in a discussion of the product Zuckerberg built and how he made it successful. In Chapter 5, we will come back to partnerships in more detail as the final principle of his success.

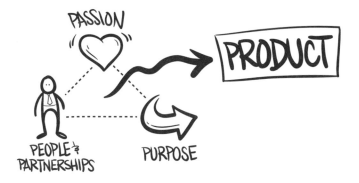

The base for the development and design of Facebook was Mark's passion and his purpose. Zuck was always passionate about understanding how people worked—a rare trait for a programmer. That is why he registered as a double major in computer science and psychology at Harvard. Addressing a large audience at BYU in 2011, he called Facebook "as much psychology and sociology as it is technology":

> All of these problems at the end of the day are human problems. I think that that's one of the core insights that we try to apply to developing Facebook. What [people are] really interested in is what's going on with the people they care about. It's all about giving people the tools and controls that they need to be comfortable sharing the information that they want. If you do that, you create a very valuable service. It's as much psychology and sociology as it is technology.[3]

People are at the center of everything that Facebook develops. Addressing their social needs digitally is what the founder (and the rest of his engineers) are interested in.

Facebook's design and its business model are aligned with Mark's purpose of connecting the world. He wants Facebook to replicate straightforward and real offline human connections online. His dedication to this vision is what made Facebook's design so clean and easy to use and its features so appealing to everyone. But his vision also brought him a lot of criticism: his obsessive focus on user experience and his pursuit of growth over money isn't seen as smart business management. Regardless, Zuckerberg continues to stick to his beliefs and, like a true captain, steers his ship in the direction he deems right.

To aid him in his journey, he puts special focus on bringing the right people on board. And the right people to him are those who share his intense passion for changing the world: "We look for people who are passionate about something. In a way, it almost doesn't matter what you're passionate about. What we really look for when we're interviewing people is what they've shown an initiative to do on their own."[4] Above all, he values passion, action, and the desire to make an impact. And he ensures that the culture he developed at Facebook provides a perfect atmosphere to make an impact.

Early on, Zuckerberg had a knack for building social programs. Some, like Facemash, might not have been entirely appropriate. Some had utilitarian value, like the program he created to help himself and others study for the "Art in the Time of Augustus" final exam at Harvard during his first semester. He hadn't been attending many classes, so he built a program where he uploaded the materials he did have and invited other class members to log in and use it as a study aid, add their images, and leave their comments. He then studied all of the uploaded information, considered others' opinions on the topics, and passed the final. Zuck wanted Facebook to also become a utility that would help people communicate through real-time connections.

He launched Facebook in his dorm room in February 2004. Zuck wasn't looking for fame, nor did he know how successful the network would become. He just got tired of Harvard's failure to create the kind of network students really desired. He and his friends would get together and talk about the need for an online world where they could all connect just like they did in real life. "Our project just started off as a way to help people share more at Harvard," said Mark. "So people could see more of what's going on at school. I wanted to make it so I could get access to information about anyone, and anyone could share anything that they wanted to."[5] Zuckerberg said that any online experience is better when your friends join in. But Zuck and his peers talked about more than just creating a social network. They talked about a world where informational transparency and the ability to share freely online would lead to great changes in the world. They wanted a chance to contribute to building that world, and Facebook ended up being the venue for them to do so.

The launch of Facebook revealed a dire need for a social network of its kind. In the first week, more than 1,000 people joined. After three weeks, more than 6,000 students, alumni, and Harvard staff were members of the network. Even though most interactions were typical of college students who like to have fun, a lot of students immediately found practical uses for the site, organizing study groups and club meetings. As it grew at Harvard, other schools began to hear about Facebook's existence and wanted in. In the summer of 2004, Zuck and several friends decided to dedicate their summer break to building up Facebook. They moved to Palo Alto, California, and started working hard on extending Facebook to multiple schools.

Just like a shrewd CEO, Mark displayed strategic thinking early on. He started by expanding into schools that already had local social networks, like Stanford and Yale. His thinking was that if Facebook were successful there, it would be easy to get other schools on board. Facebook started to take off on those campuses as well. That showed Zuck that his service had legs.

Zuck watched as other networks of the time—Friendster and MySpace—rose and fell. Friendster was primarily a dating site and fostered connections to help you find your soul mate. Friendster became popular almost overnight and had millions of users. But its success was also the reason for its failure—with so many users, the site couldn't keep up, which led to technical strains. The site became very slow and hard to use. The Friendster team was slow to respond, always saying they were working hard to add more servers, but after a while, people got frustrated and started to drop off.

Mark paid close attention to what worked and didn't for his competitors, and he learned from their mistakes and successes. He knew that rapid growth could be lethal if not handled properly. Even though he was excited about the demand (there was a waiting list of schools wanting to be added to Facebook), he wanted to be strategic about how he approached the expansion. He was very deliberate in the way he added new schools. He slowed down the process of satisfying the demand on purpose to ensure that his product and his servers could handle the influx of users. If the servers' capacity was at the max and he couldn't afford new servers, he simply waited to add new schools. It was rather ingenious. Also, every time the team upgraded the database or reconfigured the server array, they did it in a way that would accommodate 10 times more people than the site could currently handle at any particular moment. That was a highly strategic approach that proved to be brilliant. Zuck became obsessed with the performance of the site. He didn't want to share Friendster's destiny, so he was adamant about every technical detail of the site working not only smoothly but speedily as well.

In Chapter 3, I addressed the importance of correctly distributing your available resources to support your company's growth. Great leaders know when to push forward and when to pace. In the case of Facebook, Zuckerberg intuitively slowed down the onboarding of users to ensure that the technical and operational aspects of the site wouldn't break down. It was a smart move in the early stages of the firm's growth.

Rapid growth of a company, though exciting,
can be lethal if not managed properly.

Facebook's growth was unprecedented. In the first half year, Zuckerberg and his family infused over $80,000 into his start-up. Some of his friends invested as well. As the expenses mounted, the small team considered adding low-profile advertising on the site to cover the cost of servers and maintenance. Mark was focused on expanding the site's membership, and he was worried that ads might be intrusive. He looked at advertising as a necessary evil and worked to ensure that the ads would complement the social experience, not take it over. For a little while, he put a caption above the ads that read, "We don't like these either but they pay the bills."[6]

From the beginning, Facebook was just software—a platform for users to add their own information. The design was very simple, and the site was easy to use. You could upload a profile picture and add personal information such as your relationship status, phone number, AIM username, favorite books and music, favorite quotes, clubs you belonged to, classes you were taking, and more. Privacy controls were also built into the original version: you could choose who saw your information (everyone, people in your class, or people in your residential house). Zuckerberg was adamant about validating each user's identity. You could join only if you had a school e-mail address. Identity confirmation was one huge difference between Facebook and other social sites of that time.

In September 2004, Facebook added what would become one of its most popular features—the "Wall." Users could now write public messages to each other. The Wall was like a public bulletin board or a public e-mail that you could send to your friend, available for everyone else to comment on. The introduction of the feature was a response to data on users' behavior that the Facebook team had been tracking. They noted how much time users spent on other people's profiles, so the Wall seemed like a natural addition to help people connect better and share more information about themselves with their friends.

In the first several years of Facebook's existence, multiple journalists portrayed Zuckerberg and his friends as party lovers who would code all day and party all night. Mark liked to have fun just as much as any other college freshman, but he was also very focused. He knew that he needed to keep the company moving forward, and he didn't hesitate to put the rest of his colleagues on the lockdown until something got done. Early on, he showed qualities of a natural leader, according to his friends. Sean Parker, former president of Facebook, remembers: "The leader of a company needs to have a decision tree in his head—if this happens, we go this way, but if it winds up like that, then we go this other way. Mark does that instinctively."[7] Zuckerberg also made sure every angle was covered. Parker continues: "He liked the idea of Thefacebook, and he was willing to pursue it doggedly, tenaciously, to the end. But like the best empire builders, he was both very determined and very skeptical. It's like [former Intel CEO] Andy Grove says, 'Only the paranoid survive.'"[8]

Even though MySpace (with over five million users in 2004) seemed like Facebook's main potential competition at the time, Zuckerberg worried more about collegiate competition. He saw similar local networks pop up here and there on different campuses, and he devised a strategy to establish Facebook's universal dominance. As a particular network became prolific at a certain school, Facebook would make itself available not only in that school but in other schools in the immediate vicinity, thus creating a cross-network pressure that favored Facebook over the other network. Despite his age, early on Facebook's founder displayed true strategic thinking in his approach to business growth.

As the fall semester approached, Zuck and several of his colleagues decided to stay in Palo Alto and continue to build the service. By October, the site had reached half a million users; by November, it registered its millionth user and continued to grow at a rapid pace.

In the fall, Facebook introduced another new product feature—Groups. Anyone could create a group for any reason. Group pages looked similar to personal profile pages. Groups became the early version of Brand Pages and enabled brands to build student communities on Facebook. Brands saw the value not only in advertising to their target audience on Facebook, but also in building communities around particular topics. Paramount Pictures, Apple, and other brands were among the first to join Facebook for marketing purposes.

By February 2005, the site had two million active users with 65 percent of them returning to the site daily. Facebook had been deployed at 370 schools. In March, Viacom offered to buy the company for about $75 million. If he accepted, Zuckerberg would have pocketed $35 million for a year's work. This was the second offer to buy, and just as he had with the first one, Zuckerberg declined. He wasn't in this for a short-term profit; he wasn't interested in selling out.

Later that spring, the Accel Partners venture capital firm and Zuckerberg agreed on an investment deal where it would invest $12.7 million in Facebook. The deal valued Facebook at about $98 million post-investment. But high valuation isn't what drew my attention to this deal. What really impressed me was the fact that one of Zuck's demands was that Jim Breyer, Accel's co-managing partner and a shrewd investor, join Facebook's board of directors. Zuckerberg surrounded himself with smart people, and he invited seasoned veterans of Silicon Valley to join the board. He knew that he was lacking specific knowledge internally, and he wanted to bridge that gap by having access to sharp, experienced people inside and outside of the industry.

He also understood that he lacked leadership experience. He started asking questions, shadowing the best leaders he knew, and reading up on the topic. He also reached out to Steve Jobs, Bill Gates, and others who not only built their own companies but created platforms for new industries to thrive on. Zuckerberg is a sponge for learning, and he is innately curious. He doesn't shy away from admitting what he doesn't know, and he isn't afraid to ask tough questions, with "Why?" being his favorite.

As the company grew bigger and stress mounted, Zuck didn't lose his nerve. He remained calm. The bigger the company grew, the more focused he became on user experience and long-term strategy. At some point, he started carrying a little leather diary that he called "The Book of Change." On the title page, he inscribed Gandhi's quote: "Be the change you want to see in the world." The book detailed his thoughts on potential new site features, his belief on opening up the service to the whole world, and his ideas for turning the site into a platform for developers. As he and his team continued to push small and big changes to the site live, Zuck was looking ahead, building a vision and strategy for Facebook in his mind that was far bigger than just a collegiate social network.

Mark preferred to call Facebook a utility. "We wanted to build a new communications medium," said Parker. "We knew we'd be successful when we were no longer cool—when we were such an integral part of peoples' lives that they took us for granted."[9] Facebook was indeed becoming a utility for most of its users.

The team continued to innovate. They added features that resonated with users and were built for them. In 2005, they launched Facebook Photos, the photo-hosting service that took the social network to a new level. Prior to Facebook Photos, one could upload only one profile photo; Facebook Photos allowed multiple uploads. The team decided to take a gamble on the quality of the photos and compress them during the upload process so they would post faster. They also added a way for users to see not only the current picture but other pictures as well without exiting. But the biggest breakthrough feature was tagging. Facebook Photos marked the first time Facebook introduced tagging, and it was a big hit. Facebook Photos became the market leader—so much so that several years later, it was getting more traffic than Flickr, Picasa, Photobucket, and other photo-sharing services. In early 2012, Facebook reported that, on average, more than 300 million photos were uploaded to the site per day.

Why was Facebook Photos so successful when there were other superior photo-sharing products on the market? After all, Facebook Photos supported fewer file types, it had much lower resolution, and it didn't have editing features like some other services. But the ability to tag your friends in a photo trumped all of the product's shortcomings. Facebook designed a feature that was built around people and for people. Users didn't care about the quality of a photo; they cared about who was in it—their friends— and they wanted the ability to share the pictures on the go and in real time. This was eye-opening to some at Facebook and reaffirmed the direction of Mark's strategy: any online activity that was integrated into Facebook in such a way that it took into consideration the social relationships of its users was exactly what people were waiting for.

Facebook was becoming more than just a utility; it was becoming people's social graph. "Watching the growth of tagging," said Matt Cohler, Facebook's former vice president of product, "was the first 'aha' for us about how the social graph could be used as a distribution system. The mechanism of distribution was the relationships between people."[10]

The lessons from launching the photo-sharing service led Zuckerberg and the team to reexamine their data. People were obsessed with visiting other people's profiles in search of news about changes in their friends' lives. They wanted to stay more up-to-date on everyday activities of the people they cared about, but the process of visiting every profile page by page was tedious and inefficient. In another effort to give users what they wanted, the team at Facebook came up with the News Feed. Sean Parker called it the biggest technology challenge the company had ever faced. The team took eight months to develop an algorithm that selected the most interesting and relevant updates for each user based on his or her interests and behaviors. Each person's News Feed would be unique, and the content would depend on the activity of that person.

Zuck understood exactly where this product evolution would take the company. This change would be a stepping stone for future innovations he was already dreaming about. He was actively evangelizing this drastic change to the rest of the staff, some of whom remained highly skeptical.

Doubts had started to creep into the minds of some employees who questioned whether Zuck was taking Facebook in the right direction.

Besides the launch of the News Feed, 2006 was also marked by Zuckerberg walking away from a $1 billion deal with Yahoo. He somehow knew that the News Feed would be a game-changer. When someone asked him to explain why he was walking away from such an attractive offer, Mark said: "I can't really explain it. I just know."[11]

News Feed launched on September 5, 2006. Facebook engineers held their breath for the public's reaction. And they got it almost immediately—most people hated the News Feed. Protests ensued. People called Facebook's new algorithm creepy and said they didn't intend to share that much of their information with others. Protest groups appeared on Facebook demanding that the company reverse the new feature. Zuckerberg responded in a blog post: "We agree, stalking isn't cool; but being able to know what's going on in your friends' lives is. This is information people used to dig for on a daily basis, nicely reorganized and summarized so people can learn about the people they care about. None of your information is visible to anyone who couldn't see it before the changes." Zuck's reassurances didn't seem to help. There were passionate debates within the company about whether to shut down the News Feed, but Zuck didn't waver. He knew this was the right direction, and he said the fact that Facebook was where the protest groups were forming and debates were taking place was consistent with his belief in openness and his desire for Facebook to give people the opportunity to be heard. The fact that people were finding out about the existence of anti–News Feed groups on Facebook was evidence to Mark that News Feed really worked as intended, its purpose being to show users the trends and conversations around them in real-time.

When the uprising didn't calm down, the team at Facebook introduced more robust privacy controls that allowed users to have a say in what information was seen and by whom. Zuck apologized for not explaining the new feature clearly and for not introducing the controls earlier, and the protests settled down quickly. But not for a minute did Zuck consider turning the News Feed off. He knew that no matter what people said, they liked it, and he had the data to prove it. He saw people spending significantly more time on the site after the introduction of News Feed. He started to realize that people just needed time to get used to radical changes in the product. But from that moment on, he also understood that what is natural to him (complete transparency) might not be comfortable for others, a point he missed with the News Feed launch.

September 2006 became a defining month for the company for two reasons. One was the launch of the News Feed. Another was going beyond colleges and schools and opening registration to all users. This was another topic of hot debate internally. As with the launch of the News Feed, not everyone agreed that expanding beyond schools was a good idea. Some argued that young people currently active on Facebook would be turned off by the broadened demographic having access to the site. Zuck held firm in his belief that expanding the network would open up new opportunities and make the company stronger. Open registration became available on September 26, and Zuckerberg's vision and strategy yet again proved right.

The growth exploded. People of different ages and backgrounds were joining at a rate of 50,000 a day. There were no protests from current members. By the end of the year, the company passed 12 million active users. A hundred some employees watched in awe as Zuckerberg's strategy paid off and he proved himself a visionary leader. One of the employees who had opposed the News Feed recalls: "He was just two steps ahead of everybody else. He had pushed the company, and gotten lots of negative feedback. But he had been right."[12]

Thus the cult of Zuck was born. Any nonbelievers who doubted his direction felt their doubts evaporate. Those who worked hard started working even harder, elated by the vision Zuck was painting. The company's spirits, which had been shaken by the negotiations with Yahoo and by the silence of Zuck during the process, once again soared. Mark proved his status as a visionary, and he was working hard on becoming the leader his team deserved. He started communicating better and more often; he brought strong people like Sheryl Sandberg on board to complement him in areas of weakness; and he focused on building a strong culture internally and partnering with the right people both internally and externally to continue to perfect the product and grow the company.

He kept an open-door policy to ensure anyone could get access to him. He continued to dabble in coding and spent time with his engineers and designers discussing ideas. Staff liked his laid-back approach and humble attitude. One female engineer remembers that "Zuck would come into the office and, seeing every chair full, just lie down on the thin carpet on his belly, sandals flapping, and start typing into his little white Mac iBook."[13] Another female employee recalls: "We worked . . . all the time. We were each other's best friends. Work was never work for us. We worked through Christmas, over the weekends, and until five in the morning."[14]

Next up on Zuckerberg's road map: turning Facebook into a platform. Turning Facebook into a foundation for others to build software and services upon had been a vision of his for a while. According to people close to him, Zuck would talk passionately about Facebook being a platform. He would seek out thought leaders like Steve Jobs and Bill Gates, who had experience with building platforms and ecosystems, to solicit advice about his vision. Facebook Photos, as well as other social features like Facebook Events, proved the social power of user connections and people's desire to interact with friends (what Facebook calls "social graph"). Mark felt there was more the company could do with the social graph. He was ready to create a whole ecosystem around his service. "We want to make Facebook into something of an operating system, so you can run full applications," he said.[15]

It was quite an ambitious vision, one that would solidify Facebook's position as a leader. Once a whole ecosystem is constructed around your service, it becomes hard for others to compete with you. With that move, Zuckerberg could focus on creating the best possible social network for Facebook subscribers and let others layer on limitless additional services (in the form of applications) on top of the foundation he laid. Zuck's philosophy was very different from his biggest competitor at the time, MySpace, which announced that third-party applications could not operate within its network.

Facebook opened up its application programming interface (API) in 2006. API allowed users to use their Facebook credentials to log into other sites, thus making users' data available to those external parties. But before Zuckerberg publicly announced the platform in May 2007, there were plenty of discussions internally about the move. Zuck believed that the company should level the playing field for developers that would develop their applications on top of Facebook, so the decision was made to remove some of the features from select Facebook applications to support that. "We want an ecosystem which doesn't favor our own applications," the founder proclaimed. He also wanted for his new partners (outside developers) to keep the company honest with the introduction of new features and applications, so he made it possible for them to compete with Facebook fair and square. Some employees were aghast at the idea of Facebook allowing partners not only to operate on their platform for free, but also to sell ads and other services. But Zuck's vision was clear: "People can develop on this for free and can do whatever they want. They can build a business inside of Facebook. They can run ads. They can have sponsorships. They can sell things, they can link off to another site. We are just agnostic. There are going to be companies whose only product is an application that lives within Facebook."[16]

When Zuckerberg announced the platform at f8, the annual Facebook conference, he called it a movement. At that moment, Facebook was creating its own little economy online. Over 40 developers and partners were on board, some of whose applications were demonstrated at the event. People were in awe. They hadn't expected the vision to be so grand and the opportunities so vast. After the announcement, a huge public hackathon started right there at f8 that lasted over eight hours. Developers were building software on the spot, with Zuck and other Facebook engineers present. The next several days showed Facebook's leadership the true impact of what they were creating. People were installing applications and engaging with them in droves. In two days, about half a million people installed just one of the available applications that allowed users to share music. And six months later, half of Facebook's subscribers had at least one application installed on their profiles.

David Kirkpatrick, the former senior editor of *Fortune* magazine and author of *The Facebook Effect*, writes:

> The reaction to f8 across the tech industry was close to ecstatic. Facebook's platform launch became—along with the launch of Apple's iPhone a month later—one of the two most-discussed tech events of the year. No longer was it possible to dismiss this upstart as merely a plaything for college kids. The influential blog TechCrunch called the platform "inspired thinking." Prior to f8, Zuckerberg and his crew had hoped that in the subsequent year 5,000 applications might come onto Facebook and half its users would install them. But within six months 250,000 developers were registered, operating 25,000 applications . . . Facebook was becoming its own self-contained universe . . . In Silicon Valley and among techies worldwide, it suddenly became uncool not to have your own Facebook profile.[17]

Inside Facebook, a publication devoted to publishing Facebook news, stated that in 2010, the estimated aggregate revenue of external Facebook application companies was almost equivalent to that of Facebook itself—$835 million.[18] Those companies generated revenue through selling advertising and virtual goods.

The introduction of the News Feed prepared the site for the explosion of sharing. As people engaged with applications, their friends saw the news in their streams, thus providing developers with the opportunity to reach and serve more people. Becoming a platform created additional appeal for Facebook, and people continued to join in droves (at a rate of about

150,000 a day). Zuckerberg's vision and his determination to stick to his vision yet again propelled the company forward.

With the introduction of Brand and Business Pages, where people could "fan" the page versus "friending" a personal profile, more and more organizations started building their own communities on Facebook. (The Fan button later evolved into the Like button.) Not only that, brands started creating their own applications and programs to reach bigger audiences and buying advertising to drive people to their pages or offers. A lot of marketers started allocating part of their budgets to investing in online communities, specifically in Facebook communities. Marketers liked the price and effectiveness of advertising on the network as well as the awareness they got through more precise targeting options that weren't available anywhere else. Even though Facebook didn't disclose any private user information, it offered advertisers a look at key characteristics of users like demographics, location, interests, etc., all clumped together in a generic set of data. Marketers also liked having direct access to their customers and the long-term value of relationships they built with them on the platform. It wasn't just about serving ads to customers; Facebook also gave brands the opportunity to retain those customers through good content and ongoing conversations on the brands' Facebook pages, thus allowing them to build engaged communities around their brands.

Facebook Ads added a social component to the otherwise dry traditional advertising model. Ads should feature organic content, Facebook's team believed; ads should give users an opportunity to engage with the ads and with other users right inside the ad, like, for example, playing a video or seeing which of your friends liked it or commented on it. Facebook ads show how your friends interact with the ad and/or the brand, thus making it more relevant to you as a user. Facebook's ad targeting is also rather detailed: you can target users by age, interests, geographical location, gender, etc. Facebook Ads is one of the products that continues to be debated by users. Some like the fact that the ads demonstrate relevancy to people's social circles and interests, but some consider them intrusive. However, one after another, brands continue to show the effectiveness of Facebook not only in building awareness but also in increasing meaningful engagement with their customers. In 2011, comScore, Inc., a leader in measuring the digital world, released an overview of the U.S. online display advertising market for the first quarter of 2011, indicating that nearly 1.11 trillion display ads were delivered to U.S. Internet users during the quarter. Facebook accounted for 346 billion impressions (nearly double the number it delivered in the first quarter of 2010), making it the host of nearly one-third of all display ad impressions delivered.[19]

Facebook's relationship with its partners (brands, advertisers, developers) hasn't always been smooth, though. Some marketers (as well as other partners, developers, and users themselves) criticize Facebook for constantly changing the network without as much as a word to them. It becomes hard for marketers to keep up with all of the changes and sometimes frustrates users who don't experience the constant change of other social sites. Just as a brand decides to invest in the redesign of its page or works on a program with significant investment, Facebook comes out with a weighty change (for example, the Timeline—the Wall's redesign, transforming profiles into a visually rich chronology) that pushes back a company's plans and requires additional funds to implement. Some developers experienced similar frustrations with business models and strategies that heavily relied on Facebook's infrastructure. To continue to be an effective partner, Facebook needs to strike a balance between its rapidly paced "hacker way" of innovation and the needs and desires of those who not only use its product (users) but also those who sustain Facebook's revenue and growth (marketers and partners).

Finding that balance is one of Zuckerberg's biggest challenges. He admits that. "The biggest thing is going to be leading the user base through the changes that need to continue to happen," he says. "Whenever we roll out any major product, there's some sort of backlash. We need to be sure we can still aggressively build products that are on the edge and manage this big user base. I'd like us to keep pushing the envelope."[20]

Facebook has made mistakes along the way that have prompted some users to question the intentions of the company's leader. Beacon was the most dramatic mistake. Beacon was an alert system that told your friends about your buying habits. Instead of offering users an opt-in option and giving them control over what would be shared, Beacon offered only an opt-out option that disappeared after several seconds of inactivity. Some users unintentionally shared more information about themselves and their online activity than they meant to. Beacon's design flaw wasn't acknowledged by the company right away, and it was three weeks before the engineers redesigned it with an opt-in option. A while later, Beacon was shut down. That design mistake and Facebook's slow response still haunt the company. To this day, a lot of people are suspicious about Facebook's use of their information and are unsure about Facebook's resolve to protect user privacy. Zuckerberg's vision to make Facebook a hub of social information did come to fruition later on, though, when Facebook launched Facebook Connect (a Facebook log-in that allows users to log into many websites and then share their activity across the net if they choose to do so) and Open Graph API (which enables any web page to have Facebook actions integrated into it and seamlessly communicates those actions back to one's Facebook page). These features truly propelled Facebook's integration with the rest of the online world. When Facebook announced Open Graph, a lot of headlines read "Facebook Is Taking Over the Web" and "Facebook's Plan to Take Over the World."

Apple has always put emphasis on simple and elegant design. "So that's our approach," Steve Jobs told his Apple team once. "Very simple. We're shooting for Museum of Modern Art quality. The way we're running the company, the product design, the advertising, it all comes down to this: Let's make it simple. Really simple."[21] Just like at Apple, simplicity is highly valued at Facebook. Once Mark Zuckerberg described his international strategy as building "the best, simplest product that lets people share information as easily as they can."[22] The simplicity of the site is very deliberate. "We wanted to get the site out of the way and not have a particular attitude," said Aaron Sittig, who was responsible for the first major site redesign. "We didn't want people to have a relationship with Facebook so much as to find and interact with each other."[23]

Critics say Facebook's design is too simple and unimpressive. Facebook's plainness, however, is the key to the success of its design strategy. Facebook's VP of product, Chris Cox, considers design a sustainable competitive advantage. He and his team also want to recreate offline relationships online as much as possible. "The biggest thing that's different is that Facebook is not about human-computer interaction," he says, but rather about human-to-human interaction. He calls it "social design." "It's more like designing a plaza or a restaurant," he says. "The best building is one where the people inside . . . are connected. That connectivity is created by how everything is arranged."[24] Facebook is very serious about design and how users react to it. The design team's researchers work with focus groups to understand the preferences and habits of users of different demographics and cultures. They invite users to their testing center on campus to solicit their feedback. They also look at the quantitative data on how people use Facebook.

Facebook is also very focused on growth. For the past five years, the company had a team tasked with bringing new members to the site. Naomi Gleit, the second-longest-tenured employee after Zuck and a core member of the group, defines the team's mission as making "Facebook available to everyone in the world" and defines her role as growth evangelist. Her job is to remove all barriers that prevent people from joining. In 2012, the team was renamed GEM, an acronym for growth, engagement, and mobile (mobile especially has been Facebook's new priority). Facebook's concept of dedicating an entire team to growth has been copied by other tech start-ups like Quora, Dropbox, and Twitter.

The engineering team continues to perfect the product constantly. The "hacker way" respects efficiency above all. Facebook's philosophy is to "move fast and break things." The company is always looking for a way to better the service so that it takes fewer clicks and becomes more intuitive to use. Internal hackathons produced some of the best Facebook features like Timeline, video, chat, the Like button, and many more. On the eve of its

IPO, Facebook chose to host an all-night hackathon instead of throwing a party. The company will sometimes hold hackathons for its larger clients and partners to help find new ways brands can use the platform. Facebook has also found ways to export its hackathon culture to the outside world, including schools (to motivate students to think beyond the classroom). The company holds annual Hacker Cup challenges for people around the world. The competition offers a $5,000 prize and consists of five rounds of programming challenges. In 2011, it drew 12,000 programmers. Facebook also crowdsources the hacking of its own site, offering a finder's fee of $500 to $10,000 to anyone who discovers a bug in the system.

Popular slogans in Facebook's culture are:

Done is better than perfect.

Move fast and break things.

Stay focused and keep shipping.

This journey is 1 percent finished.

These slogans are displayed around the office on posters and are printed on stickers.

Charles Dowd, Facebook's employee out of Dublin, attributes the company's success to its motto: "This journey is 1 percent finished." The company puts emphasis on deployment and reiteration. Facebook ships a new set of codes each week. Developers are required to hand in their work each Sunday, and the new code goes live on Tuesday. "There is a cadence at the company that is about always moving forward," Dowd says. "Everyone at the company understands that this is how we work."[25]

Sometimes the enemy is not competition, but rather the comfort of repetition and complacency. Becoming too comfortable with current accomplishments tends to make it harder to innovate. Smart leaders avoid being blinded by the inertia of success.

> Creating an environment of agility and a sense of urgency
> is critical to the ongoing success of an enterprise
> that is looking for ways to innovate.

Knowing when to let go or when to say no is an important part of strategic leadership. In order to focus, a company cannot take on more than necessary to execute its vision and strategy. Mark Zuckerberg learned this lesson early on. When Facebook was in its infancy, Zuckerberg started working on developing new software he called Wirehog. Mark envisioned Wirehog as a service that would allow users to share content (music, video, text files) with each other. The service would be integrated into Facebook, making it the company's first application. Mark was passionate about Wirehog. Sean Parker was opposed to developing the service. He had experience dealing with the music industry in his Napster days, and he was wary of the possibility that Facebook might be accused of stealing content. Mark didn't seem to hear the pleas of his friend to drop Wirehog and focus on Facebook. Wirehog launched as an invite-only site in November 2004. The service recognized who your Facebook friends were and allowed you to share your files within your circle of connections. But Wirehog wasn't taking off as Zuckerberg predicted. The service was hard to use, and users weren't warming up to it. In the meantime, Facebook needed Mark's attention more than ever, with his coworkers working hard on supporting the growing service. Eventually, Mark made the hard decision to shut down Wirehog.

Later on, in his 2011 interview with Charlie Rose, Zuck stressed the importance of focus. Rose challenged Zuckerberg when Zuck said that Facebook didn't have any intention of going into the game-building industry. "You say that today," Rose said. Zuckerberg was adamant: no, he didn't want to get into the game-building business. He had learned his lesson:

Building games is really hard . . . We think that what we are doing is really hard and we are better off focusing on this piece. I think building a really great game service is really hard. Building a great music service is really hard. Building a great movie service is really hard. And we believe that an independent entrepreneur will always beat a division of a big company. Which is why we think that the strategy of these other companies trying to do everything themselves will inevitably be less successful than an ecosystem where you have someone like Facebook trying to build the core product and independent great companies that are only focused on one or two things doing those things really well.[26]

Sheryl Sandberg, Facebook's COO, who sat next to her boss during the interview, nodded her head in agreement. Facebook's leadership is very focused on their core business and their core purpose; they don't want to be distracted; they believe in doing one thing well. Keeping organizational focus is one of the topics Mark also discussed with Steve Jobs, who, he says, was in agreement with him on it.

> **Knowing when to say no or when to let go is a strategic quality critical for any business.**

Today, Facebook is becoming people's choice not only for connecting with friends and with brands, but also for playing games, for getting the latest news, and for shopping. Users are purchasing virtual credits on the network. In 2011, Facebook sold around $500 million worth of credits. As Facebook grows, it is expanding its payment service to various kinds of commerce. Users and organizations have started to embrace e-commerce on Facebook, or "f-commerce." Payvment, for example, is a social commerce platform on Facebook that comprises a network of over 150,000 active sellers (from small to large businesses) offering their products on Facebook. Even though f-commerce is in its infancy, it is expected to grow.

What this young CEO did right was to invest money and time into building a great product first and think about revenue second. He waited to go public until he built a solid product that set the foundation for profit in the long run. He knew that if he would have started flooding Facebook's members with ads instead on focusing on growth and reinvention, it would have alienated users (which is what ended up happening with MySpace). Too many companies place a lot of emphasis too soon on revenue generation rather than on the product itself. Steve Jobs saw Zuck's brilliance. Jobs's biographer, Walter Isaacson, says Jobs had a lot of respect for the young leader. He says the reason Jobs felt Apple didn't crack the code on social (referring to Ping, Apple's failed attempt at building its own social network) was largely because of Facebook's success. Mark did it so well, Jobs said.

Mark Zuckerberg has redefined the way people communicate and share. He has proven to be a visionary leader and a long-term strategist. He understands that to be successful, one needs to run a marathon, not a sprint. He knows that game-changing success is an endurance game. A lot of times, people who lead organizations forget that and instead succumb to the pressure of peers and stakeholders. Until leaders are rewarded for long-term thinking, persistence and patience won't be encouraged. Patience, commitment to purpose, and strategy are the key pillars in business success; you cannot reach the finish line without them. "I'm here to build something for the long term. Anything else is a distraction," Mark Zuckerberg continues to say to his critics and stakeholders.[27]

To build something amazing, or, for that matter, to continue to innovate internally, you need to make innovation personal. You need to allow your employees to not only dream up their personal inventions (big or small), but you must then provide an opportunity for them to execute on such dreams. Facebook has done that successfully, but so have others. 3M provides a perfect example of an innovative environment that allows employees to be inspired by their passions.

We have all heard about companies like Google and Hewlett-Packard allowing employees the time and encouragement to create, but it is a little known fact that 3M set the precedent for this practice years before with its "15 percent time," a program that allows anyone who works at 3M to use a portion of weekly work time to create and develop his or her own ideas. As a matter of fact, the program has produced many of 3M's best-selling products, including the Post-it note. In 1974, Art Fry, a scientist at 3M, came up with that simple but famous invention.

Founded in 1902, the company wasn't always successful. It endured years of hardship and struggled to survive. But hardship taught the company's leadership an invaluable lesson: innovation is essential for survival. Today, 3M is a multinational powerhouse, with more than $25 billion in annual sales across 50,000 products. The company holds 22,800 patents, many of which were the result of its "15 percent" program, which has been key to the company's business strategy since 1948. Kurt Beinlich, a technical director at 3M, confirms: "It's really shaped what and who 3M is . . . It's one of the things that sets 3M apart as an innovative company, by sticking to that culture of giving every one of our employees the ability to follow their instincts to take advantage of opportunities for the company."[28]

Once a year, several hundred employees from dozens of 3M divisions get together to share their ideas. They display the cardboard posters outlining their "15 percent" time projects and invite feedback as well as colleagues who would be interested in partnering with them on bringing their ideas to life. This event is highly regarded, and, as Wayne Maurer, an R&D manager in 3M's abrasives division, puts it, it is an opportunity to unleash the "inner geek." He elaborates: "For technical people, it's the most passionate and engaged event we have at 3M."[29]

Failure is accepted at 3M. Moreover, it is a part of the company's culture. You cannot immediately succeed with every invention. But you won't succeed at all if you don't try. Even though lots of companies understand that, only a small number of them truly celebrate new ideas and their exploration. Multiple companies have tried to emulate 3M's program and offer the benefit of creative freedom to their employees, and most have failed miserably in such a venture. It is expensive (3M invests over $1 billion in research and development). It also requires faith. But most companies are too conservative to support the influx of new ideas, or their culture is not shaped to support the high level of creative competitiveness required for a program like this to thrive.

This incredible benefit draws a lot of top talent to join 3M. For a true creator, no sum of money can be a substitute for the opportunity to have full freedom to work on something she is passionate about. Companies like 3M allow independent entrepreneurship within their ranks to thrive, creating intrapreneurs who revolutionize the industry and make a difference—and, in the process, contribute to the company's bottom line.

The greatest ideas can come from anywhere and anyone. A truly innovative company will find ways to champion them. Like 3M does. Like Facebook does.

> **Make innovation personal! Involve your employees,
> and give them freedom to create.**

Thomas Edison, the American inventor, who in 1879 unveiled his greatest invention—the light bulb—once said: "I failed my way to success." Edison had a substantial number of failures before he was able to produce a working prototype of the light bulb. Thomas Edison, Mark Zuckerberg, and James Dyson have a lot in common. They love a good failure—because they know it can lead to something amazing. Because ordinary is not an option. James Dyson is a British inventor, industrial designer, and entrepreneur best known for inventing the world's first bagless vacuum cleaner, the Dyson Dual Cyclone. Dyson is also known for his trial-and-error innovation approach in building function-led product designs. Just like Zuck and Edison, James Dyson prefers to invent not by theorizing but by building one prototype after another until he succeeds.

In 1978, Dyson became frustrated with the performance of the vacuum cleaners on the market, all of which eventually lost their suction. He spent five years trying to develop a functional vacuum that would be easy to use and that wouldn't have the problems other vacuums had. Supported by his wife's salary as a teacher while pumping all of his finances into the idea, on his 5,127th attempt, Dyson finally developed a working version of the new bagless cleaner. But it would take him about 15 years to launch the Dyson Dual Cyclone under his own name. Manufacturers in the United Kingdom didn't want to hear about his invention. So he launched in Japan. His first prototype, the G-Force, was sold in Japan in 1986, and in 1991, it won the International Design Fair prize and became a status symbol there. Within 22 months of launching in the U.K., the Dyson DC01 vacuum cleaner became the bestselling cleaner in Britain. In 2005, the Dyson Dual Cyclone became the market leader in the United States and the fastest-selling vacuum cleaner ever made in the U.K. The San Francisco Museum of Modern Art and eight other museums now display this breakthrough product.

Dyson says:

> I wanted to give up almost every day. But one of the things I did when I was young was long distance running, from a mile up to 10 miles. They wouldn't let me run more than 10 miles at school—in those days, they thought you'd drop down dead or something. And I was quite good at it, not because I was physically good, but because I had more determination. I learned determination from it. A lot of people give up when the world seems to be against them, but that's the point when you should push a little harder. I use the analogy of running a race. It seems as though you can't carry on, but if you just get through the pain barrier, you'll see the end and be okay. Often, just around the corner is where the solution will happen.[30]

James Dyson is on a mission to take everyday products that don't work well and make them work better. He is on a path of constantly challenging conventional wisdom. Dyson's approach to innovation is quite remarkable. He doesn't talk about ideas; he prototypes them over and over again. He says that to truly understand what works and what doesn't, one should experience it firsthand. He believes that the inventor's life is one of failure and that purposeful failure is an essential ingredient in coming up with the most breakthrough solutions. But to find the right solution, you need to look in places where you least expect to find inspiration or try out solutions that are the absolute opposite of blatantly obvious ones.

He says:

> When I was doing my vacuum cleaner, I started out trying a conventionally shaped cyclone, the kind you see in textbooks. But we couldn't separate the carpet fluff and dog hairs and strands of cotton in those cyclones. It formed a ball inside the cleaner or shot out the exit and got into the motor. I tried all sorts of shapes. Nothing worked. So then I thought I'd try the wrong shape, the opposite of conical. And it worked. It was wrong-doing rather than wrong-thinking. That's not easy, because we're all taught to do things the right way.[31]

He continues:

> We're taught to do things the right way. But if you want to discover something that other people haven't, you need to do things the wrong way. Initiate a failure by doing something that's very silly, unthinkable, naughty, dangerous. Watching why that fails can take you on a completely different path. It's exciting, actually. To me, solving problems is a bit like a drug. You're on it, and you can't get off. I spent seven years on our washing machine [which has two drums, instead of one].
>
> I made 5,127 prototypes of my vacuum before I got it right. There were 5,126 failures. But I learned from each one. That's how I

came up with a solution. So I don't mind failure. I've always thought that schoolchildren should be marked by the number of failures they've had. The child who tries strange things and experiences lots of failures to get there is probably more creative.[32]

Dyson and his team were working on a totally unrelated project when they discovered the technology that would help them produce the cold-air hand dryer that would dry your hands in 10 seconds instead of 40 and use 80 percent less energy than a warm-air equivalent. Airblade, Dyson's famous hand dryer that came to market in 2006, was born out of trial and error on a different product. It seems that this hands-on, error-filled approach works well for Dyson and his R&D team. Society, James Dyson says, is after instant gratification and doesn't reward long-term vision and perseverance but rather instant brilliance. He thinks it should be quite the reverse. Dyson's company spends large amounts of time and money on R&D (about 10–12 percent of its sales). In his products, he focuses on the utility and design above all. "It's a good thing," he says:

> Because it demands that our products are that much better. I'm a pri-
> vate company. I don't have shareholders breathing down my neck. I
> can take my time over things. Our vacuum-cleaner motor took 10
> years. Our washing machine took seven years. I'm not in a desper-
> ate hurry to get big. I'm much more interested in making interesting
> products that solve problems. That's what gives me a thrill. Getting
> big is the happy, or some might argue unhappy, result of making suc-
> cessful products.[33]

In this statement, he sounds very much like Mark Zuckerberg did before Facebook went public. Even now, Zuck is very focused on creating the best products he can possibly create above all else.

Just like at Facebook, everything Dyson Ltd. does in and around its workspace and in onboarding new hires sends a clear message that engineering is the company's priority. The workspace, which Dyson calls "campus," is set up as a learning and collaboration environment. The design and engineering floor is just a big open space that gives staff the ability to freely share ideas and talk in person instead of sending each other countless e-mails. "We want people here to feel that they're at the cusp of discovering something," Dyson says. "Normally, companies would keep R&D groups separate, so nobody knew for security reasons what was going on. But we've decided to go down the other route. There are merits in that—it sparks off ideas and people suggest things, not in their field but in some other field. But it is risky."[34] He trusts employees not to share anything that the team is working on with the outside world until it gets launched. Burned in the past by the loss of his inventions to others, Dyson puts high priority on keeping inventions secret and protecting the company's intellectual property.

Dyson's convention-defying inventions and his persistence allowed him to go from being an inventor who once relied on his wife's teaching income to a billionaire. But his approach to developing products and the insane innovation that happens within his company are more notable than the riches they brought. Dyson relies on long-term vision and his passion for overthrowing conventional wisdom to create better products and enrich people's lives in the process.

Embracing failure as a stepping stone to success and opening your mind to the possibilities of the impossible can lead to the most unexpected solutions. Look for inspiration in the least expected scenarios and situations. Pay attention to both the ordinary and the extraordinary. Don't be afraid to be naive and ask fundamental questions like "Why?" and "Why not?" Those were Steve Jobs's two favorite questions because they invited limitless possibilities; they took people outside of their comfort zone and forced them to truly create. These are Zuckerberg's and Dyson's favorite questions as well. Creativity doesn't always happen when you want it to happen, so seeking new and sometimes radically different experiences can help unleash the most innovative ideas.

> Prototyping trumps discussions. And sometimes curiosity
> and imagination trump knowledge.

There is a misconception out there that agility and innovation can happen only in the start-up world. Small companies, some say, have less bureaucracy and less management, and thus have the ability to innovate much faster than big organizations. I disagree. An intrapreneur myself, I was a part of amazing revolutions inside large companies that consistently led to reinvention. I was fortunate enough to help lead a social revolution at Intel and watch a 44-year-old company with almost 100,000 employees turn into a social business globally, ahead of many other brands of any size. I work with people every day who challenge the status quo, take personal risks to stand up for what they believe in, and define and redefine the meaning of innovation. Innovation is in Intel's DNA. It's easy to do, you may say, if your company's culture supports disruption, even welcomes it. But isn't that what culture is made of—every single one of us?

I am not the only one who shares this belief. Nancy Bhagat, VP of marketing at Intel, recently wrote a blog post on the topic and shared her own experience with innovation throughout her vibrant and successful career, which has spanned across businesses of various sizes. She writes that often people associate innovation with a start-up world and think that large companies are not capable of innovation and agility:

> My view is that our company or organization's cultures are what we as leaders decide they should be. . . .
>
> I've personally worked at large, mid-size, and tiny companies (at the smallest, I was employee number four). I have many friends that have started their own companies, or have joined other fledgling

companies. Ironically, many of my peers that have successfully driven change are from quite different environments. The reason why some people can drive change, despite employee count, is they have a deep seated desire to make a difference and don't see obstacles like company size as an impediment. Over the course of my career, I've realized that the ability to drive change is about leadership, vision and passion. It's also about executives that support you and provide the runway to drive change. Let's not forget that people play a critical role in defining the company culture too. If you want an agile, motivated workforce then hire people that are entrepreneurial, creative thinkers and action-oriented.[35]

Well said!

Being a pioneer is the hardest job of them all. Just ask Mark Zuckerberg. Changing the world requires you to be a rebel. It requires the courage to stand up to critics and to continue on the path to your purpose. Driving innovation and creating extraordinary products or services is our way to leave a memorable footprint on earth, to make an impact, even if small. Our passion defines us, our purpose drives us, and our products show the world what we believe in. What is your passion, your purpose, your product?

CHAPTER 5

PARTNERSHIPS

*I think the reason [Mark and I are] a good fit is
we spent most of our time talking about what we both
care about and what motivated us, and I could see
from Mark that what he really wanted to build
was something that fundamentally was going to change
who we are and how we interact.*
—Sheryl Sandberg, Facebook's Chief Operating Officer[1]

*Sheryl has been my partner in running Facebook and
has been central to our growth and success over the years.*
—Mark Zuckerberg, Facebook's Founder and CEO[2]

Success is a team sport. No one person can ever possibly know everything or possess all of the skills necessary to make a dream a reality at large scale. It is a natural human tendency to partner with others to reach our goals. Just as the reasons for a partnership can vary, partners themselves can take on different roles. They can be investors who contribute to the success of a venture financially. They can be employees who help a business mature by contributing their skills and experience. They can be vendors who provide the supplemental resources needed for the growth of a company. They can be spouses and family members who bring necessary emotional support during tough times. They can be friends who offer access to their networks to open up new opportunities. They can even be customers who believe in the vision of a business and are passionate about its products or services. All of these forms of partnerships are extremely important in putting together the bigger puzzle of business success and should be carefully considered and cultivated.

The kind of partnership that I want to talk about in this chapter is the partnership of imagination and execution. Not always, but very frequently, the true inventor who is able to inspire with her vision and capture the hearts and minds of people around her might not be great at the everyday mundane tasks of running a business. And those who are really great at the operational aspects of building a business might not necessarily have the technological acumen to build a product. The combinations of passions, skill sets, and motivations may differ widely, but the fact remains that the most successful businesses tend to have a leadership team whose members complement each other in capabilities and experiences. When leaders of a company share the same purpose but bring different things to the table, that is the kind of partnership that tends to be the strongest.

The Zuckerberg-Sandberg duo is an example of such a partnership. If Facebook's vast membership is purely Zuckerberg's contribution to the company's success, the business prosperity is largely the contribution of Sheryl Sandberg, Facebook's COO.

Intelligent, elegant, and highly ambitious, Sandberg arrived at Facebook in early 2008. She immediately took over the operational side of business, freeing the founder to focus on what he knows best—building up Facebook as a site and a platform. She currently oversees everything that has to do with the business side of Facebook: sales, marketing, business development, legal, human resources, public policy, and communications. With her, Sandberg brings a plethora of experience. Prior to Facebook, she was vice president of global online sales and operations at Google, where she built and managed the online sales channels for advertising as well as operations for consumer products worldwide. Before that, she served as chief of staff for the U.S. Treasury Department under President Clinton and, prior to that, as an economist with the World Bank.

Facebook's main source of revenue is advertising. Before Sandberg joined the company, the revenue grew slowly. Upon her arrival, she was able to redefine Facebook's advertising approach in line with Zuckerberg's expectations, attract a number of major advertisers, expand internationally, and become a passionate face of the company. And she is definitely passionate about Facebook. "Facebook is working every day to make the world more open and connected," she said. "It's a mission that I'm deeply passionate about, and I feel fortunate to be a part of a company that is having such a profound impact on the world."[3] Since Sandberg came onboard, Facebook's revenue has grown from $150 million to almost $4 billion.

In June 2012, Facebook announced that Sheryl Sandberg had joined the company's board of directors, the first woman to ever do so. "Sheryl has been my partner in running Facebook and has been central to our growth and success over the years," said Zuckerberg at the time. "Her understanding of our mission and long-term opportunity, and her experience both at Facebook and on public company boards makes her a natural fit for our board."[4] Sandberg currently sits on the board of directors of large companies like Disney and, in the past, Starbucks.

About four years ago, Facebook was in flux. It went through a number of major staffing changes that affected people's confidence in the company's maturity. First came the departure of Sean Parker, Facebook's president, and then the departure of Owen Van Natta, Facebook's former COO, as well as the exit of several cofounders, moves that left the outside world wondering about the stability of the business. But Zuckerberg wasn't in a hurry to fill Van Natta's shoes. He was very deliberate in his search for a replacement. When he met Sandberg at a Christmas party in 2007, his interest got piqued. In the next six weeks, an intense business courtship followed. Zuck and Sandberg met multiple times a week to talk about their various professional and personal interests. They connected. They seemed to have a very good understanding of each other's personalities, goals, and values.

Their working approach is rather effective. Every Monday morning and every Friday afternoon, Mark and Sheryl huddle to discuss the issues of the week around strategy, product, and personnel. They also touch on personal topics. "We agreed that we would give each other feedback every Friday," says Sandberg. "We are constantly flagging things. Nothing ever builds up."[5] They have also developed great understanding. "We can talk for 30 seconds and have more meaning be exchanged than in a lot of meetings that I have for an hour," Zuck says.[6] Sandberg is very protective of the young CEO. "He is shy and introverted, and he often does not seem very warm to people who don't know him, but he is warm," she says. "He really cares about the people who work here."[7] The two are also personal friends; Mark has taught Sheryl's son a few fencing moves.

"One of the reasons the company is doing so well is because the two of them get along so well," said one of Facebook's executives.[8] Another longtime Facebook executive called the partnership "a blessing from the gods." A number of Facebook's board of directors' members share this point of view. The key to the success of this relationship is the fact that Sandberg truly wants Zuck to succeed, and she is willing to take second place to him whenever necessary to support him in his mission.

Some are perplexed by this partnership. Zuckerberg is a young engineer who is socially awkward and isn't comfortable being in the spotlight. He dropped out of Harvard and doesn't have any experience in building a company. Sandberg is in her forties and is highly successful. Unlike her boss, she did graduate from college (she has both BA and MBA degrees from Harvard University); she is polished; and she is known for her interpersonal skills and vast industry connections. But I think their differences are what make the Zuckerberg-Sandberg duo such an extraordinary team. They complement each other very well. What Mark lacks in experience, Sheryl brings to the table in abundance. When he doesn't feel like stepping into the limelight, she steps in for him masterfully. The difference in age, as well as gender, contributes various perspectives and capabilities. Having Sandberg around lets Zuck fully focus on what he loves: product-building and the company's vision. He puts full trust in her running the operational side smoothly.

"The role I play is Mark focuses on building the product, and I run the business functions of the company. I really believe in what Facebook does. Technology was going to change all of our lives, and it has, but technology to power us as people is really the social networking movement," says Sandberg. "People donate their organs, people find their birth mothers, people find friends in ways they never would. And people even start movements. And I know that if I wake up and kiss my kids good-bye and come to work every day that we just might touch more people, and that really matters to me."[9] When she finishes talking, she gets teary-eyed.

When Sandberg started, she wanted to improve team dynamics within the company. Over the months, she was able to earn respect both among business-focused teams and engineers alike. During her first days at the firm, she went desk to desk to introduce herself to as many employees as she could, ask questions, request feedback, and crack jokes. She wanted to create an environment of trust and boost morale. Whenever an employee on her team gets promoted, she sends him a congratulatory note. She also spends time mentoring young employees, especially women. She is passionate about the growth of women's role in society, and she encourages young girls to be confident in going after their dreams and to not shy away from important roles simply because they may be mothers someday. In

2012, Sandberg was number eight on Fortune's 50 Most Powerful Women in Business list.[10]

Traditionally, young technology companies followed a different model of management. Even though young founders stayed on and helped the companies grow, they often preferred to bring in an established and experienced executive to run the company. They understood that those executives had the necessary skills to provide appropriate leadership, to address Wall Street audiences, and to bring operational execution and order to the start-up mentality. That was the case with companies such as Google, LinkedIn, and eBay, which recruited Eric Schmidt, Jeff Weiner, and Meg Whitman to take the helm as CEO. But it seems like the partnership model is changing, and Facebook is at the helm of that change.

Henry Blodget wrote in his article for *New York* magazine that the Zuckerberg-Sandberg partnership "has now become a new model for tech company-building. Instead of replacing the quirky founder with a professional CEO, companies now try to 'go get a Sheryl.'"[11] Jeffrey Bussgang, general partner at the venture capital firm Flybridge Capital Partners, says: "The new model is there is enough pride and recognition of the COO role when you have a young technical CEO beside you. People used to look down on that, and now it's a badge of honor . . . I think boards are just being smarter about the positive cultural impact that keeping the founder in place over the long haul can have. The founder represents the soul of the company."[12]

Facebook's model of two worlds—product development and operational excellence—integrated together and led by two people who complement each other offers an outstanding example of a company that is succeeding through strategic partnership. I call this partnership model "The Visionary and The Builder." The Visionary is the partner who is a "dream architect"—he has a clear understanding of the company's purpose and shapes its long-term strategic outlook based on that purpose; he leads the company through inspiration and blue-sky vision. The Builder is the partner who is a "value architect"—she leads the functions that support the

THE VISIONARY
DREAM ARCHITECT

THE BUILDER
VALUE ARCHITECT

mission of The Visionary and ensures that this mission is executed opera-
tionally. This is not to say that the two don't ever overlap, or that the two
partners don't share a common vision, interests, or skills. But for this model
to work successfully, as it has for Facebook, the two partners each need to
have distinguished skill sets that the other doesn't possess. In the case of
Facebook, Zuckerberg focuses on product development and the platform's
global expansion, because that is what he is great at, and Sandberg brings
operational skills that ensure stability and discipline within the company as
it executes on Zuck's vision.

The Visionary-Builder model is the most common model of partnership. Throughout history, we've seen multiple examples of partnerships that
went from two entrepreneurs and a dream to multimillion dollar empires:
Hewlett and Packard, Sears and Roebuck, McGraw and Hill. The list
goes on. But there are also instances of similar partnerships with three or
more partners contributing their wisdom, and/or their expertise, and/or
their finances to a venture. CollegeHumor, Warner Bros., and Johnson &
Johnson are among them.

Ricky Van Veen of CollegeHumor says that he learned a lesson about
the importance of strong partnerships early on. For him, he says, it wasn't
pre-planned; it just happened. And he is grateful for it. He remembers:

It started with the two of us, and then it grew to four of us for a while at the start. And it was a very lucky combination: I was the editorial and creative lead, Jake Lodwick did the programming, Zach Klein was in charge of the design, and Josh Abramson managed the business aspects. We look back in the retrospect, and we say, "How did that happen?" Though it was a strange coincidence that the four of us got together, and each of us had this specific skill set that the others didn't; it became one of the reasons for our success. We knew how to do each other's job a little bit, but not fully. Zack is one the best designers in the world, Jake taught himself how to code, and we formed this partnership—it was like each one of us was a puzzle piece, and together we made a complete picture; we fit together perfectly.

Warner Bros. was created by the four sons of Polish-born Jewish immigrants: Sam, Albert, Harry, and Jack Warner. After getting their start in the early 1900s working in film distribution (they ran a traveling movie business), they founded their own movie house and began producing their own movies. Sam came up with the idea of producing a feature-length talkie and got hold of the technology that allowed the brothers to create one. Everyone else thought it was crazy, it wouldn't work. *The Jazz Singer*, released in 1927, was a big hit and grossed about $3 million. That revolutionized the industry and put Warner Bros. on the map.

Johnson & Johnson, despite its name, was founded in 1886 by three brothers—Robert Wood Johnson, James Wood Johnson, and Edward Mead Johnson. Under their leadership, the company pioneered the first commercial first aid kits, created maternity kits to make childbirth safer for mothers and babies, manufactured the first mass-produced sanitary protection products for women, and created dental floss. In 1932, when Robert Wood Johnson II, son of the company founder, took over the company's leadership, he transformed the firm into a global decentralized family of companies and helped expand it internationally. He also wrote the company's credo, which remains the guiding philosophy of Johnson &

Johnson to this day. In 2011, the multibillion dollar conglomerate celebrated its 125th anniversary.

Steve Jobs once said: "My model of business is the Beatles. They were four guys who kept each other's kind of negative tendencies in check . . . That's how I see business: great things in business are never done by one person; they're done by a team of people."[13] The two Steves (Jobs and Wozniak) were the type of partners who complemented each other very well when they started Apple. Wozniak remembers that he would labor on his innovations while also working at Hewlett-Packard, and Jobs "would always find a way to turn them into money."[14] Even though the two of them were different, they were also similar in a lot of ways. Wozniak says: "We both grew up in the counter-culture days, we both admired people who thought differently about things . . . We were very much alike in that time frame."[15] When Wozniak unveiled his first creation—a personal computer—to his friend, Steve Jobs, he intended to give his innovation away for free. But Jobs saw the future; he shared the dream of making the world a better place through user-friendly technology, and he convinced his friend that they should start their own company, Apple Computer.

True collaboration is a powerful thing. People naturally are drawn to co-create. They want to share their ideas with like-minded people; they look for different angles and various experiences to not only help shape their ideas and make them better, but to make those ideas a reality. Alvah Curtis Roebuck, who responded to an ad for technical help placed by Richard Warren Sears, contributed his technical skills to the vision of a marketing genius—their collaboration and friendship in the late nineteenth century gave birth to Sears Roebuck and Company. But unlike Roebuck and Sears, who didn't know one another, people often find partners in their own close circle of friends and family. Trust is one of the key components in a successful partnership and is usually developed over years.

Walt Disney, whose remarkable imagination created the world of Mickey Mouse, Donald Duck, and many more beloved cartoon characters, relied heavily on his brother, Roy O. Disney, in building his empire.

Walt gave his older brother a lot of credit for building an entertainment business out of his fantasies. It was Roy who lent his brother $250 on top of Walt's $40 investment to start their partnership and open a cartoon studio. Their uncle lent them an additional $500. In the early days, Walt drew his cartoon characters, and Roy worked the cameras and kept the finances in check. Together they built an amazing empire and brightened the world for millions of kids. When Walt Disney passed away, his brother took the helm of the company. But Roy didn't try to fill the creative shoes of his sibling, stating that Walt had built a great organization and that he would keep Walt's spirit alive. Roy did not change the direction of the company, continuing the legacy of his younger brother. While Walt had a dream, Roy had the knowledge and capabilities to help his brother make his dream a reality. Roy was eight years older, had experience working in a bank, and also knew that his brother was prone to neglect his business affairs, focusing too much on the artistic side. A brilliant businessman, Roy stayed in the shadows and provided strong support to Walt as he created fascinating stories that captured the imagination of children around the world.

William Hewlett and David Packard had known each other since school. They first met in the early 1930s while studying radio engineering at Stanford University. They clicked right away. Both had a passion for the outdoors and a fascination with electronics. Shortly after they graduated, they raised $538 in start-up capital and set up shop in the car garage behind Packard's Palo Alto house. It is said that they flipped a coin to decide on the name of their venture. Hewlett won the toss, and Hewlett-Packard (HP) was born. The two men had a lot in common. They loved fishing together and hiking in the mountains. They both were avid philanthropists. And just as with other strong partners like Zuckerberg and Sandberg and Walt and Roy Disney, Hewlett and Packard saw eye to eye and shared a common vision. They were credited with creating the visionary management style, in which employees' needs take precedence above all else, and managers are given the freedom to make decisions and encourage innovation within their teams. The two leaders were much alike. Bill Hewlett put it this way:

It is important to remember that both Dave and I were products of the Great Depression. We had observed its effects on all sides, and it could not help but influence our decisions on how a company should be run. First, we did not want to run a hire-and-fire operation, but rather a company built on a loyal and dedicated work force. Further, we felt that this work force should be able to share to some extent in the progress of the company. Second, we wished to operate, as much as possible, on a pay-as-you-go basis, that our growth be financed by our earnings and not by debt."[16]

Shared values, common interests, and strong leadership collaboration put organizations like HP, Disney, and Facebook on the path to success. The long list of other examples includes Larry Page and Sergey Brin of Google, Bill Gates and Paul Allen of Microsoft, Ben Cohen and Jerry Greenfield of Ben and Jerry's, Bill Bowerman and Phil Knight of Nike, and the list goes on. These brands, recognizable across the planet, started with simple partnerships and grew into empires. The Visionary-Builder model isn't restricted to large brands, though. It works quite successfully for smaller companies as well.

Over the years, I've watched the accomplishments of the creative agency JESS3 with amazement. The team of two—Jesse Thomas and Leslie Bradshaw—grew their firm in six years from a two-person operation into a full-blown agency of over 30 people with annual revenue exceeding $5 million. What is their secret? Collaboration and close partnership. Jesse is The Visionary who started the company in the back of his room, and Leslie is The Builder who helped shape the company into one of the most-respected creative agencies in the industry.

JESS3 specializes in visual storytelling, data visualization, and rapid prototyping. And they do it very creatively. They also do specialized projects that require thinking outside the box and unique design. Their work brought them wide recognition and landed them on the cover of several magazines. In 2012, the agency ranked 430 on the Inc. 500 list. And both Leslie and Jesse were featured in Inc. 30 Under 30 that same year.

When I sat down with Leslie to talk about their partnership and asked about the role each of them has played in growing the company, she replied without hesitation: "Jesse has the vision for the company, and I have the vision of how the vision is going to get done." Then she talked about their personalities, their childhood experiences, and how the two differ: "Jesse and I overlap in two major areas: ambition and excellence. Other than that, we could not be more opposite."

Jesse is an only child; he grew up in an urban area and had many opportunities to travel thanks to his dual citizen status (New Zealand and United States) and his parents' roles at the British, New Zealand, and Australian embassies. He is a classic savant-artist type and can easily pass hours of time working alone on his creative projects. He loves pushing the limits and breaking the rules; he is bright but unconventional. He is always looking for unusual and unexpected connections. Jesse dropped out of design school to join one of his instructors in a new venture, which eventually was acquired and gave Jesse his second taste of entrepreneurship. (His first, according to school friends, involved buying gum and pencils at the store and marking them up to sell on the playground.)

Leslie is the total opposite of Jesse. She grew up in a rural environment, has a sibling, and didn't do much travel beyond the 50 states. But she played lot of sports, was very active in her community, and loved schoolwork. She values structure, discipline, compassion, and teamwork. She strives for achievement and follows the rules. At school, she was involved in student leadership and nearly every academic club on campus, and she worked with people from all walks of life. She always found herself producing something; there were always projects, deadlines, budgets, and stakeholders. She not only graduated high school as valedictorian, but she went on to earn a Presidential Scholarship at the University of Chicago and graduate Phi Beta Kappa.

The two met post-college in 2006. They were introduced to each other by a mutual friend who noticed that they both talked about the Internet a lot and thought the two of them should know each other. It was a business introduction at first, but it progressed into a long-term personal relationship. After a while, Bradshaw started helping her boyfriend with his business, eventually going full-time as president and, later, as chief operating officer of the company. Together they've taken the business to new heights. Thomas is a brilliant creative mind. "Jesse has the ability to see months and months ahead. He has a knack for predicting digital trends and has a gut feel about where the industry is going that's right more than it's wrong," says Bradshaw. And Bradshaw makes the perfect evangelist for the company. "If I believe in it, I become evangelical about it," she says. She is passionate about being authentic and delivering the best value to her customers, and that passion is contagious. I was amazed at how similar the Thomas-Bradshaw duo is to the Zuckerberg-Sandberg duo (minus the age difference).

Bradshaw believes in the importance of having several partners contribute to one another's success and goals:

> It may sound cliché, but partnership is a yin and yang. You don't want two yins, two calm personalities in a partnership. But you also don't want to yangs, two fiery personalities, either. In our partnership, Jesse is the yang, and even though I have yang in me, I have enough yin to balance it out. If you look beyond our personalities, the fact that our genders are different also adds diversity. The perspective I bring as a woman is very different from what he brings as a man, and that helps balance out the way we hire, the way we treat our employees, and the way we approach strategies when we execute for clients.

Because both partners have high ambitions and a strong drive for excellence, they do butt heads sometimes about who is in charge. Before joining forces, both were used to being number one. It is a hard balance to reach sometimes. Jesse is the CEO of the company, but Leslie is a general manager who gets things done and is accountable for operational quality on a day-to-day basis. Bradshaw stresses the importance of consensus in situations like this: "In a partnership, it is important for you at times to be willing to step down to being a number two and follow someone else's lead and at other times have the positions reversed. You need to work out with your partner what situations call for the reversal of roles and stick to the agreement. At the end of the day, you each benefit from the excellence of the other." It's important for partners to keep in mind that each partner knows his or her team best, and partners must trust one another to make the best recommendations and decisions for the business based on that knowledge.

In the six years since Bradshaw joined the firm, and in the 10 years since Thomas launched his freelance practice under the JESS3 moniker, the agency has been able to break through the noisy landscape of social media and creative agencies. The strong partnership of Thomas and Bradshaw landed them opportunities to work on innovative projects with brands like Nike, MTV, Samsung, NASA, American Express, Twitter, foursquare, ESPN, Google, and many others. JESS3 has even worked with Facebook on a number of initiatives, ranging from branding for their f8 developer conference to the original design and prototype explorations for what has become www.facebookstories.com. JESS3's f8 art was used on glass tables at Facebook's annual developer conference in 2010 and eventually on a window in its D.C. office.

We have discussed just some commonalities of successful partnerships and the personal qualities of partners that made those partnerships a success. The right business partner can multiply your chances of success, whereas the wrong business partner can be detrimental to your venture. Business partners can become your greatest asset or worst liability. On one hand, a partner can contribute manpower, diversity in skills, a different perspective and great ideas, financial resources, and networking opportunities. One the other hand, partners might clash because of different work ethics, lack of commitment, a complicated relationship, or legal and financial disagreements. It is not easy to find the right partner.

The most vibrant and fulfilling partnerships are based on a set of philosophies that partners agree upon. Those are:

1. **Clear expectations.** Partners need to be clear about their expectations of each other and about the benefits they expect to get out of the partnership. Honesty is critical here. They need to outline their roles from the start to avoid unnecessary conflict. They need to discuss the similarities and differences of their personalities and agree to deal with any issues through immediate and open dialogue. In the case of Zuckerberg and Sandberg, it is clear that the expectations were outlined up front. Zuckerberg is clearly in charge of the final decisions for the company, but he also puts full trust in his COO to make critical decisions about the company's operations, openly share her recommendations, and provide timely feedback on both professional and personal matters.

2. **Shared values and vision.** The importance of shared values and a common vision are often underestimated. If partners have different goals, the business can't grow successfully. If one is planning on

international expansion and the other wants the business to stay local, the differences in vision might lead to partners sabotaging each other. If they disagree on personal values like punctuality or philanthropy, that will have a negative impact on the business as well. Partners need to agree on the guiding purpose behind the venture they are trying to build. A huge reason for the success of HP, for example, is the fact that its founders shared the same views on how to grow the business and how to treat their employees, as well as on their financial contributions to the community.

3. **Mutual trust.** A strong partnership is based on mutual trust; it seeks to maximize the happiness and accomplishments of all parties involved. The poor decisions of one partner might affect the reputation of the other and result in financial and legal troubles. Both partners have to practice good personal and business ethics. If mistakes are made, partners have to support each other in correcting those mistakes and guiding the business to a better place. That requires not only trust but good communication and conflict management skills. Zuckerberg and Sandberg already had good rapport before they decided to work together. They spent a lot of time together to ensure they developed mutual respect and understanding.

4. **Fair exchange of value.** Partners have to contribute equal amounts of valuable contributions for a partnership to survive, including financial resources, a strong business network and connections, client lists, credentials, expertise, time, etc. Partners can work together on evaluating new ideas and business plans, offering their diverse perspectives on potential flaws; they can help each other better their ideas and shape a common vision. Partners have to work equally hard on accomplishing the same goal and improving chances for long-term success.

5. **Complementary strengths.** As we already explored in this chapter through multiple examples like Facebook, JESS3, and Disney, partnerships work best when partners complement each other. No

single person is a master of all things. The more diverse skills each partner brings to the table, the easier it will be to start, build, grow, and run your enterprise. For that fit to happen, each partner has to recognize his or her own shortcomings and weaknesses. Zuck was very open with his staff about his lack of leadership abilities early on. And later, when he brought Sandberg on board, he once again was honest about the skills the new COO brought that he didn't possess.

6. Commitment. From the start, partners need to communicate their level of commitment to the venture so that there is no animosity if one contributes less than another. Ideally, every partner is a self-motivated individual. In successful partnerships, each participant is usually personally and financially stable but relies on other partners through difficult periods the business might encounter. They hold each other accountable, which ensures that they are continuously moving forward.

7. Mutual respect. Partners need to have mutual respect for one another. Mutual respect keeps them open to constructive criticism. Establishing equality early on allows them to accept each other's opinions, feedback, and ideas. Equality means that each person's thoughts, views, and beliefs are held valuable. It means dialog rather than lecture. It means that no one person consistently dominates. Multiplicity of perspectives is what sometimes leads to the most groundbreaking solutions and most innovative products.

The partnerships discussed in this chapter exhibit all seven principles and have been successful in opening the door to incredible opportunities for both their companies and their customers. I fully expect the partnership model of Mark Zuckerberg and Sheryl Sandberg to be imitated in future years in Silicon Valley and beyond. They are a great example of the Visionary-Builder model that will set a partnership standard for generations to come.

QUI AUDET ADIPISCITUR: WHO DARES, WINS

Qui audet adipiscitur. "Who dares, wins." It seems the Latin connoisseur Mark Zuckerberg lives this motto every day.

His daring vision turned his small site into a necessity for one billion people and into a platform in and of itself, creating the whole new ecosystem around it. It is hard to imagine that just eight years ago, what we now take for granted didn't exist. Today, not being able to sign onto Facebook and share your life with your friends would seem downright odd. Facebook reported in September 2012 that it now houses 140.3 billion friendships, that 44 percent of all Internet users are now members of the social networking site, and that 600 million of one billion users are accessing the site through mobile devices.[1] Facebook aimed to mimic offline relationships online, and it is succeeding. Whether bringing their offline relationships online or vice versa, people seem to connect more than ever. The Active Network study showed in the fall of 2012 that after a social interaction on Facebook, 70 percent of survey participants said they contacted someone offline, and 40 percent stated that they met in person.[2] Facebook is now infused in every single aspect of our lives. People use the social network to connect with their close network of friends, recommend products, engage with their favorite brands, get the top news of the day, and even find jobs. Recruiting firm Jobvite found that 52 percent of job seekers use Facebook to help find work, and one in five have been sent a lead on a new job via the site. (Interestingly, the numbers were significantly higher than similar numbers for the professional network LinkedIn.)[3]

Zuck's drive to create something amazing, to "put a ding in the universe" as Steve Jobs would say, was so strong that at the age of 19, he was able to not only create but to grow one of the most powerful companies that ever existed. And yet people still have a hard time seeing past his age and inexperience. We all may have at one point underestimated him. How easily we forget that other "empires" were run by the "inexperienced." Bill Gates knew nothing about running a company when he founded Microsoft, and Amazon's Jeff Bezos had been an investment banker when he started his company in his garage. Larry Page and Sergey Brin were in college when they created Google. For some reason, it is hard for us to accept the unconventional. "Boy CEO," we called Zuckerberg. And yet he will go down in history as a kid who turned down $1 billion and spearheaded the movement toward universal connectivity.

Mark inspired a global change. He dreamed of a connected world, and he created it. He is a pioneer, and Facebook is paving the way for others in the social revolution online. When you are a trailblazer, you tend to be in the spotlight more than others, and you tend to be scrutinized more. We shouldn't forget, however, that even through his own mistakes, Zuckerberg is showing others the importance of the social graph and the right path to online transparency. Some of us might not desire or accept it right at this moment, but people change, and so do social norms. People first hated caller ID when it was introduced (for privacy reasons); now it is a feature we refuse to live without. People also didn't like Facebook's News Feed at first (for the same reasons); now it is the first thing we like to look at in the morning.

We've already seen a huge global shift in the past decade with increased sharing and the democratization of the web. Says Facebook's CEO:

> [Facebook] is shaping a broader web. If you look back for the past five or seven years, the story about social networking has really been about getting people connected. . . . But if you look forward for the next five years, I think that the story people are going to remember five years from now isn't how this one site was built, it's how every single service that you use is now going to be better with your friends. . . . People are really going to look back and say "Wow, over the last five years all these products have now gotten better because I am not doing all this stuff alone, I am doing it with my friends." That's what I am most excited about.[4]

Vanity Fair magazine ranked Zuckerberg number one on its 2010 list of the Top 100 Most Influential People of the Information Age. The same year, *Time* magazine named him the Person of the Year, stating: "In less than 7 years Zuckerberg wired together a twelfth of humanity into a single network thereby creating a social entity almost as large as the United States."[5] In 2011, Charlie Rose prefaced his interview with Zuck with: "We have entered a Facebook age and Mark Zuckerberg is the man who brought us here."[6] The fact that Facebook's CEO has changed the way we communicate online is undeniable. But some are still skeptical about his intentions. Some think that he is a scheming profiteer who is selling our personal data to advertisers to get rich. I tend to agree, though, with Lev Grossman, a journalist and a senior writer for *Time*, who put it this way: "Cynicism and greed are not character traits that appear in Zuckerberg's feature set. Facebook doesn't sell your data to advertisers. (It uses the aggregated statistics of its millions of users to more effectively target the ads it serves, but that's a long way from the same thing.) And he doesn't force anybody to share anything. The idea would genuinely, honestly horrify him."[7]

But there is a question of the company's continued growth and monetization. Facebook users now store enormous amounts of their lives on the network; that is where their friends are. So unless Facebook does something really unreasonable, I don't anticipate users abandoning the service. Facebook has over 600 million users who access the service through mobile devices; the number is growing, and mobile isn't monetized yet. Even though Facebook is late to the mobile game (and it admits it), the opportunity is still there. I am confident that the company will find the right way to capitalize on it. Brands are also flocking to Facebook in hopes of building long-term relationships with their most engaged customers. A number of global brands are finding substantial value in Facebook's ecosystem and are increasing their spend on the site. They are building large communities of fans whom they can engage with on a daily basis, thus providing an effective platform for conversations around the brand. Intel is one of those brands, with over 14 million fans on its global Facebook page, a high percentage of whom are highly engaged with that community. This is the biggest community Intel has ever been able to build, and the brand is finding it highly effective for direct interactions with customers and for word of mouth. (How do I know? Over the past three years, I led the effort of creating Intel's social networking strategy, building the communities online, and scaling those communities across geographies.)

The fact that Facebook dominates internationally is also a telling story. Facebook has taken the number one spot among social networks in most countries around the world (even overthrowing Orkut in Brazil), and it is also working hard on expanding into countries like Russia, where the local network VKontakte is still a dominant player. And who knows what Zuck's little "Book of Change" holds in terms of his future vision? Adam L. Penenberg, journalism professor at NYU and contributing writer to *Fast Company*, suggests:

> Picture, if you will, a Friday night in the near future—five, maybe 10 years from now. You head to a bar wearing your Google augmented reality glasses (with the Prada frames) equipped with speech recognition software. You're already logged into Facebook because that's the

default setting, and who bothers to change this? You scan the room, and because of Facebook's vast facial recognition database—and the fact that almost everyone on the planet has a Facebook account—you are able to identify every person in the room, and how they relate to you and your social graph.[8]

Now that Facebook is a publicly traded company, it faces the challenge of balancing the firm's focus on user value versus investors' happiness. But Zuckerberg, even though he is slightly disappointed by his company's stock price, does not seem bothered by the short-term predictions of investors; he is too focused on the long-term strategy for the company. He is looking for the right investors who share his vision and will stay with him long-term. He is in the camp with other rebels and visionaries like Jeff Bezos of Amazon, Steve Jobs of Apple, and Darwin Smith of Kimberly-Clark, who defied naysayers and revolutionized the business. In every single case, they were expected to fail.

When Amazon went public in 1997, there was a lot of skepticism about the company's ability to make money. Jeff Bezos ignored the criticism and pushed forward. Since then, he has been criticized for many other things, including pouring resources into Kindle and allowing negative reviews of books on his site. When the latter launched, people asked him if he understood his own business. But his vision was simple: if Amazon helps people make purchasing decisions, they will come back to spend more. Bezos's outlook was always long-term. "If I had a nickel for every time a potential investor told me this wouldn't work," he recalls. "A lot of people—and I'm just not one of them—believe that you should live for the now. I think what you do is think about the great expanse of time ahead of you and try to make sure that you're planning for that in a way that's going to leave you ultimately satisfied. This is the way it works for me."[9] Bezos knows that most of the time, the decision to invest in Amazon has been perceived as a risky one. But, just like Zuckerberg, he is extremely open about his strategy and welcomes every investor who believes in it as much as he does: "If you're clear to the outside world that you are taking a long-term approach, then people can self-select in," he says. "As [Warren] Buffett says, you get the shareholders you deserve."[10] To date, the vision of this leader has paid off. Amazon's compound annual growth rate of 31 percent over the past 10 years and a stock price that outperformed eBay over the same period of time by a factor of 18 is proof of that.

Steve Jobs purchased Pixar from George Lucas in 1986 for $10 million. He lost money on Pixar every quarter for nine straight years, pumping $50 million of his own money into the company. But he believed in the team and had a vision that animated movies would enrich the lives of the moviegoers. One day John Lasseter, one of the four animators then at Pixar, showed Jobs the short film he was working on. It was called *Tin Toy*. Jobs's response to Lasseter was simply: "Just make it great." *Tin Toy* became Pixar's first animated film to win an Oscar, the 1988 Academy Award for Best Animated Short Film. Pixar was acquired by Disney in 2006 for $7.4 billion. After Jobs's passing, Lasseter said: "Steve Jobs was an extraordinary visionary. He saw the potential of what Pixar could be before the rest of us, and beyond what anyone ever imagined. Steve took a chance on us and believed in our crazy dream of making computer-animated films; the one thing he always said was to simply 'make it great.' He is why Pixar turned out the way we did, and his strength, integrity, and love of life has made us all better people."[11]

In 1971, Darwin Smith became the CEO of Kimberly-Clark, a paper company whose stock had fallen radically behind the market, its survival threatened. In 20 years of running the company, he turned it into the leading paper-based consumer products company in the world, its stock beating rivals like Scott Paper and Procter & Gamble. In a bold move, Smith sold the mills and put the proceeds into the consumer business, investing in brands like Huggies and Kleenex. Wall Street called the move dumb and downgraded the stock.[12] But just like Zuck and Bezos, Smith never wavered from his course, and his long-term strategy paid off big time.

These are not the only examples of businesses that had leaders with passion, purpose, and long-term vision. And they won't be the last.

You may also remember these predictions:[13]

- "This 'telephone' has too many shortcomings to be seriously considered as a means of communication. The device is inherently of no value to us." —*Western Union internal memo, 1876*

- "While theoretically and technically television may be feasible, commercially and financially it is an impossibility." —*Lee DeForest, inventor*

- "Radio has no future. Heavier-than-air flying machines are impossible. X-rays will prove to be a hoax." —*William Thomson, Lord Kelvin, British scientist, 1899*

- "The concept is interesting and well-formed, but in order to earn better than a C, the idea must be feasible." —*A Yale University management professor in response to Fred Smith's paper proposing a reliable overnight delivery service; Smith went on to found Federal Express*

My point is that no one can predict the future. We can make educated guesses, sure. But even then, passion and a clearly defined purpose can trump any educated guess we make and deeply surprise us. The companies mentioned above are prefect examples of that. Sometimes the best strategy is faith. And it seems that visionaries like Zuckerberg, Bezos, and Jobs understand that better than anybody else. They lead with passion and vision. They trust their gut. They stay nimble and never sacrifice quality. They hire the right people to help them execute. And they find the best partners to share their journey with. They understand that overnight success can take years. They are the pioneers who have the courage to realize their long-term vision and, with it, change the world.

Nature gave each one of us the ability to be great, but getting there is the feat we ourselves are responsible for. Greatness takes passion, patience, courage, and fierce determination. And it takes action. Every little accomplishment is a step toward something bigger, and every failure is just an alteration of the path toward your dream. It is my hope that this book will give you courage to reach for the stars and pursue your dream and that the principles discussed here will assist you in getting there. And above all, have faith in yourself and in your purpose.

> *Your time is limited, so don't waste it living someone else's life.*
> *Don't be trapped by dogma—which is living with the results of*
> *other people's thinking. Don't let the noise of others' opinions drown*
> *out your own inner voice. And most important, have the courage to*
> *follow your heart and intuition. They somehow already know*
> *what you truly want to become. Everything else is secondary.*
> —Steve Jobs[14]

> *If you think you can or you think you can't, you're right.*
> —Henry Ford

NOTES

Introduction

1. http://www.facebook.com/zuck/posts/10100518568346671.

2. http://www.kare11.com/news/news_article.aspx?storyid=895807.

3. http://www.dailymail.co.uk/news/article-1252165/Facebook-lovers -married-27-years-rekindling-romance.html.

4. http://www2.nbc13.com/vtm/news/local/article/couple_with_same_first_ last_name_marry_after_meeting_online/83697.

5. http://www.mirror.co.uk/news/real-life-stories/dad-traces-long-lost-son-on -facebook-1150447.

6. http://allfacebook.com/facebook-local-restaurant_b19775.

7. https://blog.facebook.com/blog.php?post=409753352130.

8. https://blog.facebook.com/blog.php?post=409753352130.

9. Paul Adams. *Grouped: How Small Groups of Friends Are the Key to Influence on the Social Web*. Indianapolis, IN: New Riders, 2011, p.vi.

10. David Kirkpatrick. *The Facebook Effect: The Inside Story of the Company That Is Connecting the World*. New York, NY: Simon & Schuster, 2011, Kindle edition.

11. *The Facebook Effect*.

12. *The Facebook Effect.*

13. *The Facebook Effect.*

14. *The Facebook Effect.*

15. *The Facebook Effect.*

16. *The Facebook Effect.*

17. *The Facebook Effect.*

18. *The Facebook Effect.*

19. http://en.wikipedia.org/wiki/Facebook.

20. http://en.wikipedia.org/wiki/Facebook.

21. http://blog.nielsen.com/nielsenwire/global/global-and-social-facebooks
    -rise-around-the-world/.

22. http://blog.nielsen.com/nielsenwire/global/global-and-social-facebooks
    -rise-around-the-world/.

23. http://weblogs.hitwise.com/heather-dougherty/2012/02/10_key_statistics_
    about_facebo_1.html.

24. http://en.wikipedia.org/wiki/Facebook.

25. http://en.wikipedia.org/wiki/Facebook.

26. http://en.wikipedia.org/wiki/Facebook.

27. http://blog.nielsen.com/nielsenwire/global/global-and-social-facebooks
    -rise-around-the-world/.

28. http://en.wikipedia.org/wiki/Facebook.

29. http://www.socialbakers.com/countries/continents/.

30. http://www.theatlantic.com/technology/archive/2012/05/the-case-for
    -facebook/257767/.

31. http://newsroom.fb.com/key-facts/statistics-8b.aspx.

32. http://janrain.com/blog/social-login-and-social-sharing-trends-across-the
    -web-for-q2-of-2012/.

33. http://newsroom.fb.com/key-facts/statistics-8b.aspx

34. http://weblogs.hitwise.com/heather-dougherty/2012/02/10_key_statistics_
    about_facebo_1.html.

35. http://www.zdnet.com/blog/facebook/facebook-accounts-for-1-in-every
-7-online-minutes/6639.

36. http://newsroom.fb.com/key-facts/statistics-8b.aspx.

37. http://techcrunch.com/2012/07/26/earnings-call-facebook/.

38. http://newsroom.fb.com/key-facts/statistics-8b.aspx.

39. http://newsroom.fb.com/key-facts/statistics-8b.aspx.

40. http://royal.pingdom.com/2012/06/18/how-many-sites-have-facebook-in
tegration-youd-be-surprised/.

41. http://weblogs.hitwise.com/heather-dougherty/2012/02/10_key_statistics_
about_facebo_1.html.

42. http://weblogs.hitwise.com/heather-dougherty/2012/02/10_key_statistics_
about_facebo_1.html.

43. http://www.independent.co.uk/news/people/profiles/mark-zuckerberg-hes
-got-the-whole-world-on-his-site-2034134.html.

44. http://www.forbes.com/sites/onmarketing/2012/05/21/move-over
-entrepreneurs-here-come-the-intrapreneurs/.

Chapter 1

1. http://www.deseretnews.com/article/700121651/Mark-Zuckerberg-speaks
-at-BYU-calls-Facebook-as-much-psychology-and-sociology-as-it-is
-technology.html?pg=2.

2. http://theweek.com/article/index/227963/the-new-york-times-mark
-zuckerberg-profile-4-intriguing-revelations.

3. The Facebook Effect.

4. http://www.fastcompany.com/1693257/facebook-drama-social-network
-wont-show-you.

5. http://nymag.com/news/features/zuckerberg-family-2012-5/.

6. The Facebook Effect.

7. http://en.wikipedia.org/wiki/Mark_Zuckerberg.

8. http://spectrum.ieee.org/at-work/innovation/facebook-philosophy-move
-fast-and-break-things.

9. http://fastcompany.com/node/1822794/print.

10. http://articles.businessinsider.com/2010-10-26/strategy/30087593_1_
passion-entrepreneurs-business-advice.

11. http://www.readwriteweb.com/archives/mark_zuckerberg_inspiration_for_
facebook_before_harvard.php.

12. *The Facebook Effect.*

13. *The Facebook Effect.*

14. http://www.moviemaker.com/directing/article/jim_jarmusch_2972/.

15. *The Facebook Effect.*

16. *The Facebook Effect.*

17. *The Facebook Effect.*

18. http://www.engadget.com/2012/02/01/zuckerberg-outlines-idealistic
-facebook-mission-in-ipo-filing/.

19. http://www.macstories.net/roundups/inspirational-steve-jobs-quotes/.

20. *The Facebook Effect.*

21. http://www.fastcompany.com/1784824/great-tech-war-2012.

22. Srully Blotnick. *Getting Rich Your Own Way.* New York, NY: Jove
Publications, 1982, p. 58.

23. http://www.incomediary.com/how-to-think-like-warrenbuffett.

24. http://www.quoteswise.com/estee-lauder-quotes.html.

25. http://www.time.com/time/specials/packages/article/0,28804,2036683
_2037183_2037185,00.html.

26. *The Facebook Effect.*

27. http://www.facebook.com/notes/michael-novati/thoughts-on-openness/
475945144483.

28. *The Facebook Effect.*

29. http://news.stanford.edu/news/2005/june15/jobs-061505.html.

Chapter 2

1. http://www.history.navy.mil/wars/kearsage.htm.

2. Simon Sinek. *Start with Why: How Great Leaders Inspire Everyone to Take Action.* New York, NY: Portfolio Trade, 2011, p. 41

3. Ibid.

4. http://www.michaelgalpert.com/post/140737454/the-many-faces-of -facebook.

5. *The Facebook Effect.*

6. http://www.fastcompany.com/node/59441/print.

7. *The Facebook Effect.*

8. http://www.wired.com/business/2010/05/zuckerberg-interview/all/.

9. http://www.engadget.com/2012/02/01/zuckerberg-outlines-idealistic -facebook-mission-in-ipo-filing/.

10. http://www.fastcompany.com/node/59441/print.

11. http://www.deseretnews.com/article/700121651/Mark-Zuckerberg-speaks -at-BYU-calls-Facebook-as-much-psychology-and-sociology-as-it-is -technology.html?pg=2.

12. http://www.time.com/time/specials/packages/article/0,28804,2036683_ 2037183_2037185,00.html.

13. http://www.time.com/time/specials/packages/article/0,28804,2036683_ 2037183_2037185,00.html.

14. http://www.time.com/time/specials/packages/article/0,28804,2036683_ 2037183_2037185,00.html.

15. http://www.time.com/time/specials/packages/article/0,28804,2036683_ 2037183_2037185,00.html.

16. http://www.wired.com/business/2010/05/zuckerberg-interview/all/.

17. http://www.webpronews.com/facebook-now-has-a-billion-active-users -zuckerberg-compares-it-to-chairs-2012-10.

18. http://www.huffingtonpost.com/blake-mycoskie/fulfilling-my-lifes-missi_ b_362589.html.

19. http://www.youtube.com/watch?v=Xlp1Pa1WKgM.

20. *Fortune*, January 24, 2000. http://money.cnn.com/magazines/fortune/for- tune_archive/2000/01/24/272277/.

Chapter 3

1. http://nymag.com/news/features/mark-zuckerberg-2012-5/.

2. http://www.gallup.com/poll/150383/majority-american-workers-not
-engaged-jobs.aspx.

3. Tony Hsieh. *Delivering Happiness: A Path to Profits, Passion, and Purpose.*
New York, NY: Business Plus, 2010, p. 137.

4. *Delivering Happiness,* p. 134.

5. Joseph Michelli. *The Zappos Experience: 5 Principles to Inspire, Engage, and
WOW.* New York, NY: McGraw-Hill Companies, 2011, p. 49.

6. *Delivering Happiness,* p. 184.

7. http://blogs.wsj.com/digits/2012/02/01/mark-zuckerbergs-best-quotes/.

8. *Delivering Happiness,* p. 97.

9. *The Zappos Experience:,* p. 46.

10. http://www.fastcompany.com/1822794/boy-ceo-mark-zuckerbergs-two
-smartest-projects-were-growing-facebook-and-growing.

11. http://money.cnn.com/2012/01/04/technology/facebook_hacker_cup/
index.htm.

12. http://tech.fortune.cnn.com/2012/03/06/how-to-get-a-job-at-facebook/.

13. http://tech.fortune.cnn.com/2012/03/06/how-to-get-a-job-at-facebook/.

14. http://www.fastcompany.com/1822794/boy-ceo-mark-zuckerbergs-two
-smartest-projects-were-growing-facebook-and-growing.

15. http://www.fastcompany.com/1822794/boy-ceo-mark-zuckerbergs-two
-smartest-projects-were-growing-facebook-and-growing.

16. http://www.tumblr.com/tagged/andrew-bosworth.

17. *Triumph of the Nerds.* PBS documentary. DVD. Directed by Paul Sen. 1996;
New York: Ambrose Video, 2002.

18. http://blogs.hbr.org/taylor/2011/02/hire_for_attitude_train_for_sk.html.

19. http://blogs.hbr.org/taylor/2011/02/hire_for_attitude_train_for_sk.html.

20. Gary Vaynerchuk. *The Thank You Economy.* New York, NY: HarperCollins,
2012, p. 91.

21. *The Thank You Economy*, p. 90.

22. *The Zappos Experience*, pp. 159–160.

23. *The Facebook Effect*.

24. http://www.fastcompany.com/mic/2010/profile/facebook.

25. http://www.fastcompany.com/mic/2010/profile/facebook.

26. http://www.tumblr.com/tagged/andrew-bosworth.

27. http://www.fastcompany.com/mic/2010/profile/facebook.

28. http://spectrum.ieee.org/at-work/innovation/facebook-philosophy-move
    -fast-and-break-things.

29. http://www.fastcompany.com/mic/2010/profile/facebook.

30. http://www.insidefacebook.com/2007/07/09/insider-perspectives
    -ex-googler-justin-rosenstein-on-making-the-jump-to-facebook/.

31. http://mashable.com/2012/03/09/faceook-mobile/.

32. http://mashable.com/2012/03/09/faceook-mobile/.

33. http://www.businessinsider.com/why-young-employees-quit-their-jobs
    -2012-9?utm_source=twbutton&utm_medium=social&utm_campaign=
    careers-contributor.

34. *The Zappos Experience*, p. 258.

35. http://www.fastcompany.com/3002197/why-employees-big-dreams
    -should-be-your-companys-top-priority?utm_source=feedburner&utm_
    medium=feed&utm_campaign=Feed percent3A+fastcompany per-
    cent2 Fheadlines+ percent28Fast+Company percent29&utm_content=
    Google+Reader.

36. http://en.wikipedia.org/wiki/Dale_Carnegie.

37. http://bps-occupational-digest.blogspot.com/2012/09/laugh-and-workplace
    -laughs-with-you.html.

38. *The Zappos Experience*, p. 240.

39. *Delivering Happiness*, p. 151.

40. http://www.intelfreepress.com/news/intel-tattoos-speak-volumes/.

41. *Start with Why*, p. 111.

42. http://osxdaily.com/2011/10/06/steve-jobs-narrates-the-crazy-ones/.

43. http://www.ifoapplestore.com/db/10th-anniversary-poster/.

44. Vince Lombardi. *What It Takes to Be #1: Vince Lombardi on Leadership.* New York; NY, McGraw-Hill Companies, 2001.

45. http://www.newscientist.com/article/dn17277-male-hummingbirds-break -speed-record-for-love.html.

46. http://www.fastcompany.com/1822794/boy-ceo-mark-zuckerbergs-two -smartest-projects-were-growing-facebook-and-growing.

47. http://www.nytimes.com/2010/10/03/business/03face.html?pagewanted=all &_moc.semityn.

48. http://www.fastcompany.com/1822794/boy-ceo-mark-zuckerbergs-two -smartest-projects-were-growing-facebook-and-growing.

49. http://www.businessinsider.com/steve-jobs-mark-zuckerberg-walter -isaacson-fortune-brainstorm-2012-7.

50. http://www.nytimes.com/2012/05/13/technology/facebooks-mark -zuckerberg-at-a-turning-point.html?pagewanted=all.

51. *The Facebook Effect.*

52. *The Facebook Effect.*

53. http://www.time.com/time/specials/packages/article/0,28804,2036683 _2037183_2037185,00.html.

Chapter 4

1. http://www.independent.co.uk/news/people/profiles/mark-zuckerberg -hes-got-the-whole-world-on-his-site-2034134.html.

2. http://www.quoteswise.com/estee-lauder-quotes.html.

3. http://www.deseretnews.com/article/700121651/Mark-Zuckerberg-speaks -at-BYU-calls-Facebook-as-much-psychology-and-sociology-as-it-is -technology.html?pg=all.

4. http://news.byu.edu/archive11-mar-zuckerberg.aspx.

5. *The Facebook Effect.*

6. *The Facebook Effect.*

7. *The Facebook Effect.*

8. *The Facebook Effect.*

9. *The Facebook Effect.*

10. *The Facebook Effect.*

11. *The Facebook Effect.*

12. *The Facebook Effect.*

13. *The Facebook Effect.*

14. *The Facebook Effect.*

15. *The Facebook Effect.*

16. *The Facebook Effect.*

17. *The Facebook Effect.*

18. *The Facebook Effect.*

19. http://www.comscore.com/fre/Insights/Press_Releases/2011/5/U.S._ Online_Display_Advertising_Market_Delivers_1.1_Trillion_Impressions_ in_Q1_2011.

20. *The Facebook Effect.*

21. Walter Isaacson. *Steve Jobs.* New York, NY: Simon & Shuster, 2011, p. 78.

22. *The Facebook Effect.*

23. *The Facebook Effect.*

24. http://www.fastcodesign.com/1669366/facebook-agrees-the-secret-to-its -future-success-is-design.

25. http://mashable.com/2012/03/09/faceook-mobile/.

26. http://www.youtube.com/watch?v=LFdUEkTzDeI.

27. http://www.fastcompany.com/59441/facebooks-mark-zuckerberg-hacker -dropout-ceo.

28. http://www.fastcodesign.com/1663137/how-3m-gave-everyone-days-off -and-created-an-innovation-dynamo.

29. http://www.fastcodesign.com/1663137/how-3m-gave-everyone-days-off -and-created-an-innovation-dynamo.

30. http://content.dyson.com/insidedyson/.

31. http://www.fastcompany.com/76673/failure-doesnt-suck-part-2.

32. http://www.fastcompany.com/59549/failure-doesnt-suck.

33. http://www.fastcompany.com/76673/failure-doesnt-suck-part-2.

34. http://www.wired.co.uk/magazine/archive/2011/11/features/the-seventh
    -disruption-james-dyson?page=all.

35. http://blogs.intel.com/marketeer-musings/2012/10/11/does-size-matter/.

Chapter 5

1. http://www.youtube.com/watch?v=LFdUEkTzDeI.

2. http://newsroom.fb.com/News/Facebook-Names-Sheryl-Sandberg-to-Its
   -Board-of-Directors-182.aspx.

3. http://newsroom.fb.com/News/Facebook-Names-Sheryl-Sandberg-to-Its
   -Board-of-Directors-182.aspx.

4. http://newsroom.fb.com/News/Facebook-Names-Sheryl-Sandberg-to-Its
   -Board-of-Directors-182.aspx.

5. http://www.nytimes.com/2010/10/03/business/03face.html?pagewanted
   =all&_r=0.

6. http://www.nytimes.com/2010/10/03/business/03face.html?pagewanted
   =all&_r=0.

7. http://www.nytimes.com/2010/10/03/business/03face.html?pagewanted
   =all&_r=0.

8. http://www.nytimes.com/2010/10/03/business/03face.html?pagewanted
   =all&_r=0.

9. http://www.makers.com/sheryl-sandberg.

10. http://money.cnn.com/magazines/fortune/most-powerful-women/2012/
    full_list/.

11. http://nymag.com/news/features/mark-zuckerberg-2012-5/index4.html.

12. http://www.foxbusiness.com/technology/2012/05/18/get-me-sheryl
    -facebook-coo-model-to-be-mirrored/.

13. http://en.wikipedia.org/wiki/Steve_Jobs.

14. http://appleinsider.com/articles/12/05/10/steve_wozniak_interviewed_about_apple_steve_jobs_technology.html.

15. http://appleinsider.com/articles/12/05/10/steve_wozniak_interviewed_about_apple_steve_jobs_technology.html.

16. http://www.hp.com/retiree/history/founders/hewlett/quotes.html.

Qui Audet Adipiscitur

1. http://mashable.com/2012/10/05/the-most-important-facebook-number-140-billion/.

2. http://www.mediapost.com/publications/article/184044/social-media-interactions-may-influence-offline-be.html.

3. http://mashable.com/2012/10/09/jobs-facebook-linkedin-twitter/.

4. http://www.youtube.com/watch?v=LFdUEkTzDeI.

5. http://www.time.com/time/specials/packages/article/0,28804,2036683_2037183_2037185,00.html.

6. http://www.youtube.com/watch?v=LFdUEkTzDeI.

7. http://www.time.com/time/specials/packages/article/0,28804,2036683_2037183_2037185,00.html.

8. http://www.fastcompany.com/1843130/facebooks-social-pivot.

9. http://www.evancarmichael.com/Famous-Entrepreneurs/959/Lesson-5-Dont-Chase-the-Quick-Buck-Think-LongTerm.html.

10. http://www.evancarmichael.com/Famous-Entrepreneurs/959/Lesson-5-Dont-Chase-the-Quick-Buck-Think-LongTerm.html.

11. http://news.cnet.com/8301-13579_3-20116912-37/with-pixar-steve-jobs-changed-the-film-industry-forever/.

12. http://business.highbeam.com/392705/article-1G1-19194403/battle-bottoms.

13. http://www.rinkworks.com/said/predictions.shtml.

14. http://mashable.com/2011/10/05/steve-jobs-quotes/.

INDEX

ABOUT THE AUTHOR

Ekaterina Walter (Portland, OR) is a social innovator at Intel. A recognized business and marketing thought leader, she is a regular contributor to *Mashable*, *Fast Company, Huffington Post,* and other leading-edge print and online publications. Walter has been featured in *Forbes* and *BusinessReviewUSA* and was named among 25 Women Who Rock Social Media in 2012. She was a featured speaker at TEDx, Web 2.0 Summit, South by  Southwest Interactive (SXSW), MIT Leadership Forum and other major national and international events. Walter sits on a Board of Directors of Word of Mouth Marketing Association (WOMMA) and is an active member of the Thunderbird Global Council at Thunderbird School of Global Management. Find Ekaterina on Twitter: @Ekaterina or her blog Building Social Bridges (http://www.ekaterinawalter.com).